Antigua Marine Survey & Consulting, Inc.
DBA/ Two Can Sail
454 Gaspar Key Lane
Punta Gorda, Fl. 33955

Two Can Sail

The "5 Step Plan" to Buy a Boat to Go Cruising!

Written by Captains
Jeff Grossman
& Jean Levine

Copyright
© 2015 Jeff Grossman and Jean Levine, Antigua Marine Survey & Consulting, Inc. dba Two Can Sail. Except as provided by the Copyright Act, no part of this publication may be reproduced, stored in a retrieval system or transmitted in any form or by any means without the prior written permission of the authors.

All photos in this book were taken by the authors except as noted. All subjects in the photos printed in this book have given written consent for use, although their names are not noted.

Printed in the United States of America
First Edition 2015
Second Edition 2016
ISBN 978-1-36-474965-1

Questions regarding the ordering of this book or for assistance in obtaining your dream yacht contact us. info@TwoCanSail.com

Find out more about the Five Step Plan on our website.
www.TwoCanSail.com

Meet Captains Jean Levine and Jeff Grossman
at any of the follow boat shows.

Strictly Sail Miami, sponsored by the
National Marine Manufacturers Association

Annapolis Boat Show, United States Boat Shows
Annapolis, MD

Southwest International Boat Show, Houston, TX

*We would like to dedicate this book
to the hundreds of couples we have
helped through this educational
process and who are now
members of our worldwide
Two Can Sail cruising family.*

*Special thanks to you all
for paying it forward
to our next fleet
of new sailors.*

Table of Contents

1. Why the Five Step Plan is designed for couples......................12
2. What couples need to know to buy a boat to go cruising.........14
3. How long should it take to complete the Five Steps 15

STEP 1 Sample The Lifestyle
1. Why you need to sample the lifestyle before you buy...............23
2. How your perspective will change with life aboard..................26
3. Male and female different points of view.................................27
4. What you should learn on your first live aboard cruise............30
5. How to choose a school to take formal sailing lessons............40

    Checklist Step 1..50

STEP 2 Get Time on the Water
1. What you can do to get more sea time......................................54
2. Chartering on your own and visiting new places......................59
3. Learning how to be Captain...62
4. Getting to know a boat that is new to you.................................63
5. The 10 things to test on charter that will help you
   choose the right boat to buy..65
6. New destinations to explore and what you can learn...............72

    Checklist Step 2..78

STEP 3 Buy the Right Boat
1. How to choose and buy the right boat......................................82
2. The factors to consider before you shop for the boat..............82
3. Top 10's interior, exterior, electronic features.......................106
4. Insurance and financing your dream boat..............................114
5. What you need to know about the purchase process..............116
6. Why you should choose a broker and surveyor......................116
7. The next 10 things you need to do..126

    Checklist Step 3..129

STEP 4 Learn Your Boat
1. How to get familiar with your boat.................................132
2. Understanding your boat's systems and equipment..............139
3. What you need to know about Chartplotter, VHF, etc...........152
4. Safety equipment, a guide...158
5. What you should know about the outboard and dinghy........160
6. Test your knowledge on this systems checklist..................163
7. Recommended cruising equipment list............................164
8. Checklist to see if you are ready to go............................171
9. How to select vendors to work on your boat.....................173

    Checklist Step 4 180

STEP 5 Get Advanced Training
1. The additional training you need..................................184
2. Why you need navigation training.................................186
3. Navigation skills checklist...191
4. Why you want to learn how to interpret weather...............192
5. Test your weather knowledge with this checklist...............203

    Checklist Step 5..204

Summary
1. Example of a couples first voyage.................................208
2. Samples of couples out cruising....................................220
3. A review of the Five Step Plan.....................................227
4. What our clients say about us......................................236
5. About the authors..239

The author's Skye 51 flying five sails.
(This Photo as well as the cover photo taken by Nana Bosma)

ACKNOWLEDGMENTS

Our heartfelt thanks go to all who supported us as we started Two Can Sail, opened doors for us in the industry, and helped us give birth to this book:
Dave Amann (Sailing Florida Charters);
Bob Bitchin' (Cruising Outpost);
Steve Bowden (Sea-Tech Systems);
Lee Chesneau (Weather by Lee);
Liza Copeland (Author);
George Day (Bluewater Sailing magazine);
Peter Durant (Sail America),
Meredith Laitos (Editor at large);
Paul Jacobs (U.S. Sailboat Boat Show, Annapolis, MD.)
Ed Massey (Massey Yacht Sales);
Kevin Murphy (National Marine Manufacturers Association) and Peter Trogden (Weems & Plath Marine Supply Annapolis, MD.)
Harold and Margie Ochstein (Couples Cruising Classes)
Brenda Wempner (American Sailing Association)
We also offer warm thanks to our friends and couples that have helped with this book; Diane Allen, Steve Honour, Margaret and Jim Nelson, Jim and Bev Slager, Ian and Cindy Smith.
Of course, thanks to our families,
editors and sisters Barbara and Cathy,
and especially Jeff's Mom, who survived all of his sailing adventures as a young man.

Forward

Pick the most idyllic picture from one of those sailing magazines you have piled on your coffee table. Now, imagine yourself in that picture.

We wrote *TWO CAN SAIL* to help ensure you are in that picture and that you are still smiling long after the photo is taken. Adapt our Five Step Plan to your sailing style and goals and you can enjoy sunset cocktails, at anchor, in your own cruising boat off the island of your choice.

The best way we know to bring points to life is through stories that illustrate lessons we learned through our many years of sailing, teaching and cruising. Although we were both sailors, we started out at different skill levels and over time, we learned to work together as a couple. We evolved from racing sailors to cruising sailors; it is through this background that we developed our Two Can Sail business.

We guide couples through our five step plan from attending our couples cruising seminar at boat shows, lifestyle cruising instruction as American Sailing Association instructors or our "Try a Cat" sailing experience. We continue as guidance counselors and buyers brokers from shopping for that dreamboat, through the survey and buying process. Then after the purchase through personal training aboard the couples new boat, we help them transition from land lover to live aboard cruiser.

Once you head out on your own, we assist with voyage planning and first Gulf-stream crossings, connecting to our on the water network of other past graduates until you are flying solo with confidence.

We have designed this book to be read by couples that may have partners at different skill levels. We share our communication tips that will help you build confidence and develop the teamwork you need to sail together in harmony.

It's also designed so that you can easily jump back to check if you missed something as you progress through the five steps. The checklists throughout the book allow easy skimming of parts where you just want to refresh your knowledge.

We differentiate between facts and opinions when we teach. Facts are things that all sailors agree on. Opinions are just that, views based on our experiences and tastes. For example, some people prefer mono hulls and some people prefer catamarans.

The opinions we express here are drawn from decades of experience in sailing, cruising, teaching, and voyage training with couples. However, we encourage you to get other opinions. Compare them. Try them on for size. See which best fits your needs and style.

This couple sailing happily together into the sunset.

Why the 5 step plan is designed for couples.

Just about everyone we've met, regardless of age or walk of life, can learn to sail, learn to cruise, find a boat that meets their budget, and sail away and come home some day with their relationship still thriving.

We have always enjoyed teaching sailing, doing it for free in our spare time for most of our lives. However, when we were cruising in the Caribbean, we were saddened by how many unhappy cruisers we encountered. Many of the couples we met had taken sailing lessons, but failed to understand the systems on board. A surprising number of couples just bought the boat and took off completely unprepared.

This is why we formed our company, Two Can Sail, and developed techniques specific to couples sailing. Couples sailing differs significantly from two pals sailing together because of the emotional investment a couple brings to the experience.

Both of us learned to sail in our youth and progressed through the operation of many different size boats, from dinghies up to our Skye 51' cruising boat. Our seamanship skills and our ability to fix and maintain boats grew over a long period of time.

We often use true stories to illustrate our points, just about everything that can happen out there has happened to us or to one of our close friends. We have found folks learn better when we use stories to teach a particular lesson and they find it more fun. Throughout this book, we will share tales of "Two Can Sail" couples (with their names changed to protect the innocent) in hopes that you will find a couple whose experiences ring true for you. We focus on the unique relationship a committed couple brings to cruising. In this book, we will refer to male and female couples (what He's thinking versus what She's thinking), but there is no reason this shouldn't apply to any couple, it's the relationship and the different expectations that committed couples bring to this venture that matters. The vast majority of boats out cruising are sailed by couples, just two aboard, but most available training is oriented to crewed boats. These couples don't want to frighten, endanger or bully each other at sea. They want to be genuine partners equally excited and equipped to make this the shared adventure of a lifetime.

We hope our "5 Step Plan" will help you come to love the cruising life together. Dreams do come true!

What couples need to know to buy a boat to go cruising is the basis for the 5 Step Plan.

The 5 Step Plan is a guide to the things you need to learn to go from dreamer to cruiser with someone you love while avoiding needless, possibly dangerous, drama along the way.

The five steps are broken down into bite size segments and within each step is a checklist of skills and experience that you will need to successfully go cruising and stay together as a couple.

We encourage you to use the checklists at the end of each step to check off the things you already know. Then, research the things that you do not know, learn them, and check them off, and move on to the next item on the list.

Having a plan will keep you both smiling!

How long should it take to complete the Five Steps?

We can't give you a time frame. Every couple is unique. We have seen couples successfully go from zero through the five steps, happily cruising on their own boat, in one year while others have spread the five steps over many years.

Two Can Sail allows you to tailor the learning pace to match your time and budget and, most importantly, to fit your relationship.

We are sometimes asked how much it will cost to follow this Five Step Plan. Some couples fear this will take funds from their cruising/boat purchase kitty.

We assure you that however much time and money you spend following these steps will be far, far less than what you will end up spending, in dollars and in emotional costs, if you do not!

Boats and their systems can be expensive in dollars, time, or both; and mistakes are often measured in thousands, or even tens of thousands, of dollars. Many joke that B.O.A.T. stands for Bring Out Another Thousand, so we call one thousand dollars "One Boat Unit."

Take this path to learning and it will save you many, many Boat Units in the long run! And it might even help save something priceless – your relationship with each other.

Why shouldn't we just buy a boat and go?

Time, money and your relationship

What could go wrong.....

California Dreamers

Example: *This is one sample of what could happen with no training or experience; we'll call it the just go method. One couple from California dreamed of sailing in the Florida Keys, so they flew to the Keys and bought a 1969 36' C&C sloop, a simple vessel with very basic systems. Using all their savings they paid $29,000 cash.*

They moved aboard in May, and by July of the same year, they were ready for divorce. They had not realized that the Keys in the summer are hot, buggy and there is very little wind for sailing, the cost of a slip is very expensive, and safe places to live at anchor are limited. With no air conditioning aboard, they were miserable. When the reality of living aboard in the Florida Keys did not measure up to the dream, they put the boat up for sale and it eventually sold for $12,000.

They had to continue to pay the expenses of owning the boat, while praying they could get someone to buy the boat at any price. This story actually ended well for them, as they were able to sell the boat before they completely ran out of money.

This couple might have considered an alternative to the outright purchase of a boat; perhaps a sample cruise of the lifestyle in advance of the purchase could have saved them money, time and their marriage.

Boat Shows are where dreams often begin. Try attending a show near you and chart your course on a smooth path to your goal.

You can live the dream no matter what your style, whether it on a mono-hull, catamaran or even a trawler.

Catalina 42

Lagoon 410

Selene 43

**Sample the Lifestyle.
Learn to Sail.
Attend Seminars.**

The right sailing vacation feeds the dream!

STEP 1 Sample the lifestyle

Why you need to sample the lifestyle and learn to sail before you buy a boat.

Step one involves changing your mindset from dreaming to action. You already know goal setting is the key to success in your work life. Now, before you run out and buy a boat, you need to set suitable goals. That begins with learning the reality of boat ownership and cruising.

Can you remember the last time you spent the night on a boat? Have you both slept aboard before? One of the key factors for couples today is the comfort factor. And we mean psychological, physical and financial comfort that suits your relationship, your ages, your fitness and your budget.

That's why we suggest that you sample the life style by choosing a trip on a boat like the one in your dreams but with skilled crew to guide you. This may be the cruise that convinces a reluctant spouse or partner to sign on for the adventure.

Diane finds her inner sailor.

Example: *Diane & Dan began to plan their escape about one year before they were ready to retire.*

Dan, as a young man in his twenties, set off to sea as crew on a 100+ foot yacht voyaging through the Caribbean and then later through the canals of Europe. He had fond memories of places he would like to revisit. Diane comes from the sailing town of Annapolis, Maryland and has watched many a beautiful yacht sailing along the shore. She once owned a small 16' boat of her own.

But careers and life took them away from the water for many years. They knew they would need to practice their sailing skills. Diane liked the idea of living aboard and going cruising, but was still unsure how they should proceed. They attended our Couples Cruising Seminar at the Miami Boat Show, where all those attending shared their dreams. While at the show, they looked at various different boats and narrowed it down to a mono hull.

For Step One, to refresh their sailing skills, Diane and Dan chose a live-aboard class in the Florida Keys in March, one of the most ideal times to sail there.

Dan & Diane are now retired and out cruising.

The water was calm and translucent, a gentle breeze blew and as Diane did yoga on the foredeck, she had an epiphany. She realized not only "I can do this" but "I want to do this."

After their week long sailing class, living aboard and cruising around the Florida Keys, Diane and Dan agreed this was the life they wanted in their retirement.

How your perspective will change with life aboard.

All of your life has been full of things to accomplish on a schedule, such as schoolwork and family obligations. Life on a boat is very different, steered by where and when the weather takes you. So you and your partner each need to consider your mindset. Will both of you be able to let go of your busy scheduled life? Cruising is a lifestyle change.

Accept that making a change does not come easy and most of all, it must come from you. You need to want to make that change. Your relationship as a couple will evolve.

Your decision to live aboard a boat and go cruising will also depend on your relationship: some people are leaders, some are followers, and sometimes the roles get reversed. A partnership that has the ability to reverse who leads and who follows grants you both the freedom to make a lifestyle change like this.

The experience of living together on a boat tends to act as a magnifying glass to the relationship. If the relationship has real issues to start with, these issues will likely be magnified until one of you is off the boat. If the relationship is good to start with, it gets deeper and stronger! Ask yourselves: "Can you can adapt to changing situations?"

Like the birds in nature, part of us wants to build a nest. Think of the boat as your new nest that will go with you wherever you are. You may sell your land home, but you can still keep your sense of home. So ask yourself, why do you want to live aboard a boat and go cruising? Is it for the adventure of seeing what lies over the horizon or to feed your soul by visiting new places and meeting new people?

You each can have a different reason for wanting a lifestyle change, but you need to decide together how you can both get what you want from the experience.

The male and female points of view or Venus & Mars factor (What's in it for *me*?)

Each of you should ask yourselves: "What do I want to get out of this experience?" Write down your answers and then share them with one another and compare. This should start from the very first time you begin the discussion about the possibility of living on a boat. This should also open up more questions and concerns that you can talk about. In this way you can reach a mutual decision of how, when, and if, to proceed.

Maybe "he" thinks cruising would mean freedom from job stress, the challenge of man versus the elements, harnessing the wind and then harpooning Moby Dick. Okay, maybe just fishing off the back of the boat is his dream. But that is as far out as "he" has thought.

Maybe "she" thinks cruising would mean visiting all those beautiful tropical islands she has read about in the magazines, lounging on a beach reading a book or snorkeling and seeing swaying colored fans and soft coral gardens.

Or, is one of you thinking: "It's just an endless list of chores" with fears and questions: "How do I do laundry? Who will fix what breaks? How do we stay in touch with the kids or grandkids? What about groceries? What about bad weather?" We could go on with the list, but we think you get the idea.

Discussion of these fears will help you move from the "you want to do what?" stage to telling your friends about your shared dream.

The right trip will give you both a real life experience. This is the time to take a week aboard a crewed yacht and see in person how you both react and find answers to many of those questions. It will make you a better-educated consumer, able to narrow down the multiple choices of boats and see through all the marketing glitz to focus on what you really want.

You both need the desire to do this, and there is no better way to build that desire than to have a great experience.

A monohull in the Bahamas

A Catamaran in Belize

What to experience and learn on your live aboard lifestyle vacation.

Maybe you picture yourself on a beautiful sunny day with crystal clear skies above, a light breeze kissing your face as you glide through turquoise waters in quiet tranquility aboard a yacht. As you sail along the coast, you pass slowly by a beach of white sugar sand, nestled in a small cove. You pick out a secluded spot and drop anchor. After enjoying some well-deserved rest, you venture on to a new island and explore a small village where the locals welcome you with rum drinks served in a coconut shell. So far it sounds great!

Do you really think the locals are topless tropical beautys serving you umbrella drinks as soon as you hit the beach? What is it really like? Like all things in life, both good and bad can be found, so before you go and spend hundreds of thousands of dollars on a boat, perhaps you should investigate further.

If you don't both return home from this experience with a strong desire to do more, there's a message in that. Cruising may not be the life you imagined as a couple.

Do you have any thoughts about choosing a monohull or a catamaran? If you already know that you don't like the boat leaning over heeling, then you may want to try a catamaran. If you are a little older, not as fit as you used to be, you could consider a trawler. Maybe you are already thinking about just cruising along the Intracoastal Waterway (ICW), so why not try out the cruising life on a canal boat on the Erie Canal.

Next, consider both your current physical fitness and health. If you have good balance and sufficient strength to haul up the sails, a more active sailing adventure might be for you. But you must base the decision on the least fit member of the couple. This is important so that you can both participate in the activities aboard; after all, if you do choose to buy a boat, you will both need to be able to operate it.

Now, pick an appropriate destination. Just as you make decisions based on both your fitness levels, you choose the destination based on both of your combined sailing/boating experiences.

Perhaps he has sailed several times with friends who needed racing crew, but she has only been out on a sunset cruise once and felt queasy. He loved the feel of the boat heeled over with the rail in the water and spray coming over the deck; she was uneasy with the boat heeling. Based on this information, choosing what we call a "Level One" location would be best until the party with the least experience can get more comfortable on board a boat. Examples of Level One locations are the British Virgin Islands or the Abaco Islands in the Bahamas. These areas feature short sailing days in protected waters each with their own flavor.

If you both have been sailing and perhaps even taken some formal lessons and feel comfortable on board a boat at sea, then consider a Level Two destination such as Antigua, Guadeloupe, Tahiti or Tonga, to experience open water sailing. Some of the islands are very remote, so you will learn more about having limited resources.

If you already have twenty days of sea time under your belt, have a good understanding how to navigate, and feel comfortable on a boat in open water, try Level Three locations. Level Three locations would include: St. Vincent and the Grenadines, Greece, and the Seychelles. These locations provide challenging open water sailing conditions; require more than basic navigation skills, good anchoring techniques and the skills to Mediterranean moor.

Sailing in Greece offers a chance to practice Mediterranean mooring

Most important of all, when you ask each other where in the world would you like to go, do you both have the same answer? Pay attention to your answers; this matters as you may already have very different ideas about what the cruising life will be like for the two of you.

Pick the right time to sail.

Once you have a destination in mind, seasons and typical weather make a difference in your timing. The Caribbean is a year round destination, yet the winds vary over the course of a year.

You should consider the typical wind speeds for certain times of the year to help you decide when to sail. In springtime, the winds are lighter; therefore, it is easy sailing for the novice. Summer is Hurricane season, but early in the season, like July in the British Virgin Islands, can be a great time with fewer crowds and warmer water temperatures for first time snorkelers to delight in seeing tropical fish and colorful corals. In the winter, the winds will be stronger, but the temperatures will still be a delightful break from that of North America, so winter is a great time to use your holiday vacation time to explore the possibilities.

The Mediterranean is best in late spring until fall. The Pacific Northwest is definitely a summertime destination. Places down under, like Australia and New Zealand, have the opposite season, so winter is spring/summer and vice versa.

Use the Internet to check the average temperatures and rainfall averages to help narrow down locations. Each of you should write down three places you would like to go, and then see which ones overlap.

What a fun way to decide where to go first, second and third!

Now, think about your crew.

You want to sample the lifestyle with a couple and not just a single captain. A single male captain may relate with the male side of the couple but may not understand the hidden fears of the female, or she may not be able to express her concerns to a stranger. Likewise, a single female captain may also not be able to relate to the man, so choose your crew wisely. You'll have a chance to observe the dynamics of how a couple works together, including how they cooperate, how they resolve conflicts and how they share responsibilities. A regular crewed yacht experience may be a lovely vacation, but you will be shielded from various aspects of boating that you need to witness first hand to see both the good --- and not so good --- aspects of living aboard.

So ask about the captain and crew, learn how long they have been together cruising and whether they will share what they know with you. Most charter companies have a description of the crew that goes along with the yacht; just ask for their resumes.

Here are a few key things to observe from your cruise.

Think about something as simple as cooking aboard. Whichever partner is the cook of the family will have questions about how to cook in the small (by our land home standards) galley. Provisioning in a foreign port is always very different from mainland North America. Go with the crew to shop at the local food store and watch how they stow it all on the boat. You may not have even thought about what you do with the trash. How big is the refrigerator and how does that compare with the storage you have at home now? Where does the trash go? Provisioning is just one example of things to which you want to be exposed before you start shopping for a boat.

Another example is the refrigerator. The refrigerator runs off the batteries, so opening the door of a side-opening refrigerator lets the cold air out and causes the motor to turn on, thereby using more power to operate. A top-loading fridge keeps the cold in, so it is more efficient. This is one example of how the boat's battery capacity could affect your comfort and the way you live. Ask the crew what they need to do to charge the batteries to keep the fridge running.

You will be amazed at how much you can absorb by watching what the crew does and how their communication works while docking and anchoring.

What to expect: fun, sun and adventure, with a touch of education thrown in for good measure. If you have never been out of North America, it's always good to visit a new country with experienced cruisers who will help you navigate in a foreign port.

You should have exposure to different cultures and learn what to expect. You should also experience living with limited resources, and managing with what you have aboard in order to establish a base line to compare comfort and livability of different boats. Be observant while on the live aboard cruise. Think about the difference between how you lived on the boat during the week versus how your life is ashore now. This will help you decide if you want to continue the pursuit of living aboard or just want some retreat from the rat race every now and then. The compromise may go something like this: "Okay, honey, instead of a circumnavigation, let's charter boats in different locations around the world."

Charter ownership programs are just an example of another way you can purchase a boat sooner rather than later, and get your "hands on" sea time. You can utilize this program to travel the world and get a sample of places you want to return to when you are full time cruisers.

You may even decide that this is really your cruising style: to fly to Tahiti, sail around for a few weeks and let someone else take care of the maintenance. After five years, sell the boat and go on another adventure.

**A Moorings 46' Catamaran
a great choice for this family!**

Example:
Carl and Cindy were successful business owners. After many years of hard work, they franchised their business, which gave them both time and money to pursue their sailing dreams. They took a one-week basic sailing to bareboat charter course aboard a catamaran, in the British Virgin Islands (BVI) and loved it. Afterwards, they attended the Miami Boat Show where they were introduced to the Moorings Charter ownership plan.

Excited to gain more experience they bought a Leopard 46' catamaran in the Moorings program, which allowed them up to twelve weeks (per year) over a five-year period to sail in the BVI. This program gave them the ability to get more sea time and training.

Over the next three years, they used all their allotted charter time sailing the boat. They sought out more training and practice so they could do more and venture beyond the Caribbean. They took additional advanced training on navigation, and exchanged their charter time in the BVI for different locations, such as Tonga and Thailand.

How to choose a school to take formal sailing classes.

Think back to when you learned to drive a car and you had to take a six week drivers education class, then practice behind the wheel, pass a written test and demonstrate that you could drive the car to a DMV examiner. Then ask yourself if you would consider learning to fly on your own, with a book in your lap, or learning from your friend down the road who took one flying lesson?

For some reason, the respect that the sea deserves is not given in the same way as the respect for the air is given. Yes, the Air is more unforgiving than the Sea, but the Sea can still provide a great deal of "entertainment." Hopefully, you are reading a lot as you delve deeper into the world of sailing and cruising.

Many of the tales and books written tell of the drama that the writers experienced as they figured everything out on the fly. Remember, the authors who wrote those books about just going and figuring it out on the fly are the ones that survived. There are many, many more who just took off and failed. They may have gotten divorced, sold the boat in a foreign port, wrecked the boat or lost their lives. Those who failed don't write books.

Make sure you're both pulling the same way!

Over the decades we have watched countless guys (sorry to stereotype here, but it's almost always the guys that do this) buy a boat with almost no experience, refuse any training, pile the wife, and sometimes the kids aboard, and take off crossing the Gulf Stream to Bimini. More often than not we'd meet him down island somewhere sailing solo and divorced. Maximize your chance of a successful experience for both of you, treat the endeavor with the respect it deserves and take lessons.

We strongly recommend you learn from professionals at an accredited sailing school. There are several entities that offer a whole path of learning. The American Sailing Association (ASA) and U.S. Sailing. Colgate's Offshore Sailing School is associated with U.S. Sailing and provides their certifications. By far, the ASA has the most schools and locations and it is much more focused on the lifestyle of cruising. U.S. Sailing claims to be the governing body of the sport of sailing in the United States.

Forgive us for a gigantic generalization: in our experience, men learn better from men, women learn much better from other women and couples learn best from other couples! As you choose a sailing school, look for one that can work with the needs of both partners, as individuals, and as a couple.

The Venture 22 is a lot like this Macgregor 25

Example from Jeff:
I didn't start sailing actively until around age 12 with my dad on a Rhodes 19. We had so much fun that two years later, dad bought a Macgregor 22 (a.k.a. Venture 22). We named it "Ranger" and sailed frequently from the mooring field in Miami's Coconut Grove to Florida's Upper Keys. My dad was ex-Coast Guard and taught me all my navigation and seamanship. However, he was new to the "tender" ways of the Venture. In this context, "tender" means she heels easily in gusts and can't carry a lot of sail in a breeze.

On one of our first sails, Mom and my sister, Cathy, were sitting on the low side when a big gust hit and heeled us so far over water poured over them into the cockpit. Dad and I quickly released the sheets and Ranger came back upright, but that was it for Mom and Cathy's sailing.

Neither of them ever willingly went sailing again.

Choosing a school.

Since we are ASA instructors, we'll focus on and review the ASA path, but please note the other entities offer similar structure and are quite good as well. In the end, like all education, it comes down to the quality of the individual instructor, and the dedication of the student.

The ASA path starts with 101 sailing. You will find it is a bit like learning a foreign language, since everything a sailor touches has to have its own name. We call the first morning session "what do you call that" time. Often the words or names come from a legacy of sailing thousands of years old. When we tell the story of why something is called what it is; our students enjoy the learning more and find they remember it better.

For example, when facing forward on a boat, the left side is "port" and the right side is "starboard." This is a legacy from the days when sailors couldn't put holes in their boats and still keep them afloat; hence, they couldn't stick a rudder under the boat. Instead, to steer they strapped a board to the side of the boat. Since most humans are right handed, the "steering board" was strapped to the right side. When the boat came into a port, it had to put its left side to the dock so as not to foul the steering board. Thus, the left side of the boat became known as the port side and the right side the steering board side, which over the millenia got warped to port and starboard.

After learning the basics of the terms and how a sailboat works, you progress until you receive your "driver's license" for chartering (renting) a boat on your own. You can continue the progression with an excellent, though challenging, Navigation class and Advanced Coastal Cruising, which gets into nighttime operation, heavier winds and handling emergencies.

If you are planning on buying your own boat and going cruising, these advanced courses are very valuable and should be mandatory. Many of the schools today offer a "zero to hero" program, that is, from basic sailing to basic cruising to bareboat charter certification in a week. Please, do not do this. They do not tell you the cram course is like drinking water from a fire hose and they push you to get as many certifications as possible.

At some point, you will be told that no matter what your previous experience, after a one week "zero to hero" course, you'll be able to charter a boat in the BVI. This is probably true, since the joke in the industry is "You only need two things to charter in the British Virgin Islands; a pulse and a credit card."

Assuming you are starting at or near zero, you can get through all the course material and pass the three tests in one week, but you will not know how to sail. If you really wish to learn to sail, then spread it out. Take the basic sailing course in two to three days. Then get some sailing experience. Take the basic coastal cruising (103) and go sailing. Then, come back and take the bareboat chartering (104) in at least three days. Instead of asking how many certifications you can get in a week, slow down the pace and ask what kind of boats the school teaches on and how old they are.

Ask about what the weather conditions are like during the time you want to take classes. Of course, you cannot nail down the weather far in advance but asking if it is the rainy season or what temperatures to expect may help you choose the location of the school. Ask about the instructors and if they have taught couples. These other details can help you make your decision. If you take one class, say ASA 101 Basic Keelboat Sailing and the boat turned out not so nice, or you didn't connect with your instructor, you will have a different boat and instructor at a different location for the next class. In addition, you will have the benefit of sailing two different boats in two different locations.

Many of the schools out there also have charter fleets with boats you can take out on day sails. For example, Sailing Florida Charters in St. Petersburg, Florida has a fleet of over 20 boats ranging from 29' to 53'. You can take a five day 101/103 course and then day sail on your own one of their 30-35' boats and get real experience. We've seen classmates from the course get together for the day sails to support each other.

We'd love it if everyone would set a goal of 100 hours on the water before running out and buying a boat. You can translate that into five-hour average day sails over twenty days or three weeks of charters. If you take your three weeks on different boats then you will really understand the differences and be a better judge of what features you want on the boat you buy. Every hour of on-the-water experience allows you and your partner to gain confidence and piloting skills.

No matter where you learn to sail, keep one goal always in mind: Don't scare the spouse! Drama is a dream killer.

Use a concept called "effortful learning."

The easiest way to explain the concept of "effortful learning" is through example. Jeff began learning to play guitar his senior year in high school and continued to learn for the first few years of college. But after 40 years Jeff plays at exactly the same level as when he graduated college, not a lick better. No effort has been put into improving his guitar skills in the past 35 years. (Jeff's piano playing has gotten a lot better though!) Jean had been sailing most of her life, but never really raced. When she moved to Florida, she started racing in the all-women's regattas, where there were several women who always dominated the fleet and had been doing so for 20 years. Jean then joined our friend Steve as crew on his boat for the regular racing season. Steve is an outstanding racer, good enough to have qualified and competed in the Sunfish World Championships. Jean spent three years in intensive, effortful learning at the "Steve School of Racing," then came back to the women's Bikini Cup Regatta and blew the doors off the other women. Though they had been racing much longer, they had put no effort into improving and expanding their skills.

Sailing is an infinite body of knowledge.

We put a great deal of effort into improving our skills for the past four decades or more, and there is still much more for us to learn. Mastering the cruising life requires ongoing effort. If you keep growing your skills, you will find the experience one of the most rewarding things you will ever do in you life.

Attending Boat Show seminars will also advance you education, here is a sample seminar agenda.

Annapolis Boat Show Couples Cruising Seminar

9:00   Getting Together: Planning Your Dream.

9:30   The Five Step Plan to Your Dream and the Waypoints to Get You There.

10:00 *Short Break*

10:15 How to Choose a Boat: what factors to consider to make it easy for just two.

11:30   The Cruising Lifestyle: what's it really like?

12:30   *Break for Lunch*

1:30 The Budget Basics: examples of living expenses and boat choices.

2:30   Equipment Alphabet: GPS, VHF, AIS, SSB, what you need.

3:15   *Short Break*

3:30   "The Fear Factor" Let's talk about our fears: emergencies at sea, sailing at night; open water passages, bad weather.

4:00   "How to Stay Happily Afloat": tips on teamwork

5:00 – 5:30 Question & Answer Session

You should attend boat shows and continuing education seminars.

Going to boat shows helps expose you to new technology and advancements in the industry as well as provides an opportunity for attending the vast number of seminars they offer. General topics like basics on rigging and sails; batteries and solar power options; or even docking and anchoring techniques are offered and taught for the price of a show ticket in the form of one-hour lectures and even on the water classes.

More in depth seminars are also given during the show for anywhere from $60 a session to $495 a session, by various experts in the marine industry. Full day courses on diesel engines, refrigeration, weather and our Couples Cruising seminar helps fill in the questions you have now learned to ask after basic sailing classes.

Checklist

1. You share a live-aboard experience for at least one week.

2. You both master formal basic sailing lessons, boat terminology, on the water sailing skills, upwind tacking, jibing downwind, reaching and man overboard practice.

3. You both understand the "Rules of the Road".

4. You both know what is United States Coast Guard (USCG) required safety equipment, and what additional basic equipment should be on board, such as: compass, anchor, first aid kit, VHF radio, etc.

5. You have mastered basic communication skills on the VHF radio. You both understand how to make or respond to a distress call.

6. You both understand anchoring and mooring techniques.

7. You both have basic chart reading skills and can use a chartplotter.

8. You both have docking and line handling skills.

9. You both understand the operation of basic systems on board, such as the engine, the head and the galley.

10. You both know where to get local tide and weather information.

Resources - where to go to learn STEP 1

American Sailing Association (ASA) 310-822-7171
www.american-sailing.com

U.S Sailing 401-683-0800
www.ussailing.org

Offshore Sailing School
(Colgate Sailing School) 239-454-1700
www.offshoresailing.com

Womanship
 (Focused on women only classes) 1-800-342-9295
www.womanship.com

Royal Yachting Association (RYA)
www.rya.org.uk

Boating Safety Classes:

United States Coast Guard
www.uscgboating.org

United States Power Squadron
www.usps.org

Live Aboard Sailing Vacations

Two Can Sail: Life Style Charters
www.TwoCanSail.com

Mooring Yacht Charter
www.moorings.com

Get time on the water

STEP 2 Get more sea time

Crew on a boat for a racing season and advance your skills.

What you can do to get more sea time.

There is nothing that can replace time on the water. Many activities require a certain number of hours before moving to a higher level. Like flying and scuba diving, they require a log of these hours to document that the experience is appropriate to the task being attempted. Here are our suggestions for getting more time-on-the-water experience, sometimes for free or with a small investment.

Volunteer as racing crew

In the Tampa Bay area, there are several clubs that welcome anyone with an interest in sailing to join in as crew for regattas. Check out your local clubs and sign up as crew for the "Beer Can" races (less formal races, just for fun), usually held on a weeknight after work throughout the spring/summer.

At first you may be what we call in racing "rail meat", meaning you sit on the rail to help flatten the boat's angle of heel. When the crew tacks, you scamper over the cabin top to the high side and resume sitting on the rail. After a while, you may be called upon to hoist and trim sails. The best part is you get to learn from others' successes and mistakes, and it may only cost you the price of bringing the lunch or a six-pack of beer.

Join a Boat Club

Check into various fractional ownership companies: for example. WindPath is Catalina Yachts' part ownership program, where one person owns the boat but eight people share time and expenses of the boat. SailTime is Beneteau Yachts equivalent program; the price varies according to yacht size and location, but it is a very good sample of what yacht ownership will be like at a fraction of the cost of buying your own boat. Plus, it gives you a chance to get more sea time.

Join a sailing or yacht club

Try to find a club that is proud of its sailors. Very often, the club owns a number of small sailboats or dinghies that are available to use on a first-come first-served basis, free to its members. Pictured on page 58 is a fleet of small boats available for use to any of the guests at this resort in Antigua. Many yacht clubs have similar fleets available and host a variety of classes for free with your membership. You can get involved as race committee or run a support boat, learn a lot and have fun.

A good example is a Precision 19' trailer sailor

Buy a Small Boat

If you are the type of person who feels that you must learn on your own, then go ahead and buy a boat. This is not the one and only cruising boat, but a simple, small first boat to help you get your sea time, an inexpensive boat, with a price of less than $20,000. Small trailer sailboats are a good start; they can be sailed on lakes if you are inland and they can be easily stored on the trailer in the winter. Some suggestions are the Catalina 16.5, Compact 19, Flying Scot, Precision 19 or the Santana 23. If you live near the water, then you can consider a boat with enough volume for camping out, like the Macgregor 26, Catalina 30 or a Watkins 33. These boats have the basic systems: a motor (gasoline outboard or inboard diesel), water tankage and a head. You will gain valuable experience just owning a small boat and be surprised that even the simplest boat requires maintenance and costs money.

Then get out on the water; not only do you learn from your own sailing but you learn from others around you. As we have said before, among Jean, Jeff and our best friends, if it can happen, it has probably happened out there to one of us during our lifetime of sailing.

Example: *Here's what we learned from our friend Paul. Our sailing club hosted Friday evening beer can races that started in Clearwater Pass, went once around a Mark (about a mile out) and back to the finish in the pass. One particular evening, the wind was quite gusty, making it a challenge to go around the course with just two people, like many of the boats were doing. Paul was sailing his canary yellow Mirage 19' swing keel trailer sailor named "Loose Caboose." A sudden gusty swirl caught their jib, spinning them suddenly and pinning the two of them on what was now the low side, with the boat heeling so severely that water was rushing over the cockpit coaming, flooding the cockpit and sinking the boat.*

Here comes the lesson learned: The Mirage was designed for lake sailing and had a companionway notch that went all the way down flush level with the cockpit floor. This meant any water getting into the cockpit flowed into the cabin. They did not have the hatch boards in when they took the "spinning knockdown" and all of that water flowing into the cockpit went straight into the cabin. Paul had just enough time to tie a lifejacket to a line and tie the line to a stern cleat as a buoy marker before the boat sank under 20' of water. This is an example why we suggest doing the crazy stuff in a race where there are lots of other boats around! Within minutes, a friend on a 45' boat came up and plucked the two of them out of the water. Paul called a salver to raise his boat back up. The next Friday evening beer can race Paul was back out with his canary yellow boat ... but it had a new name, "Yellow Submarine"! He won that night's race so when he went to get his trophy we all had to break into song singing choruses of "We all live in a Yellow Submarine."

Lessons Learned:
Always protect the companionway from water getting in. When the weather picks up, put the hatch boards in. Pick a boat suited to your intended use.

This is also why we like to suggest what we call the graduated length method, begin with a smaller simple boat, and then move up to your desired cruising boat. Because what you have time and money for now may not be the same as when you retire. Maybe joining a boat club or part time ownership club will not only give you a sample of sailing but also, an understanding of the expenses that come with boat ownership.

Lasers, Beach Cats and other small boats are a great way to get started.

Chartering on your own and visiting new places

To get experience and sail different boats, you should bareboat charter. If operating a boat with you as the captain and giving instruction to your crew sounds a little intimidating, don't worry! That is why the flotilla was created.

On a flotilla, you will have a guide boat that you will follow so you can focus on your boat and, perhaps, on getting yourself and your crew more confident in the sailing and the systems.

You will have the security that knowledgeable assistance is nearby, yet not on board, so you can be independent. You may want to do your first bareboat charter from a location you have already visited on a previous occasion. Depending on the location and your flotilla leader, you should have a blend of set itinerary, assistance with minor mechanical difficulties and practice with VHF communications, as well as social activities.

You can find flotillas in various ways through charter companies and local sailing schools. Another benefit to joining a flotilla for your first charter is that a captain that sails those waters regularly has local knowledge and can even lend a hand for your first docking experience at a new marina or help keep you off that sand bar.

Don't forget to check the tide.

Here is another quick short story that has to do with knowing about the tides and what time it's coming or going and how that will affect your day.

Way back in the '70's, long before cell phones, Jeff's Mom was to pick up his Dad late in the afternoon at Coconut Grove Sailing Club (CGSC) following his day sail. His Mom waited for a while at the club and became worried. A club member suggested they try hailing Dad from the VHF that they kept behind the bar. Mom reached Dad on the VHF and he told her that he was waiting for Clyde to come, and when Clyde got there, they would be sailing back. Mom didn't know who Clyde was or why Dad was waiting for him before coming back. It turned out Dad was aground on a sandbar waiting for the tide not someone named Clyde.

Lesson learned: *Often times when you are grounded on a sand bar, your best tactic is to just patiently wait for "Clyde."*

Check the tide and pick the right spot!

Example: *We lead a flotilla in Pine Island Sound on the West Coast of Florida. As part of the support we provide, we give a detailed chart briefing as to where we will sail and anchor for the night; then we help each boat get off the docks.*

On one flotilla, we departed last and because we had the fastest boat in the fleet, we knew we would be able to sail by the fleet of eleven boats and shoot some photos as we sailed. From our vantage point, we could see one of our boats off to the south heading right for a sand bar, so we made a quick call on the VHF, and they changed course.

We led the fleet into the anchorage for the evening. There was an uneven bottom in the anchorage, but plenty of room for the eleven boats in the flotilla. One of the boats had picked a spot that was, shall we say, not a good choice. Because of our local knowledge, we cued them in and they moved over a little.

The next morning they noticed another boat had come in during the night and was sitting aground on the very spot that they had originally chosen.

Tip: follow the leader but never stop navigating your own boat.

Learning to be Captain.

Example first bareboat charter as captain:
Jean here: My perspective really changed when I suddenly found myself as the responsible party. Bareboat chartering a boat is not like renting a car; not only is the boat you are renting worth ten times the dollar amount of a rental car, but it is also someone else's home. Just think about it: if a guest spilled red wine on your white counter top and did nothing to clean it up or to try to get the stain out, you would be upset.

So I had to remind the crew to be respectful of others' property and treat this boat like it was their own boat for the week. After all, we signed a contract that grants permission to use the boat and we are financially responsible.

Oh Captain, My (new) Captain!

Practice your captaining skills by sailing different boats in different locations, where you make the call of how things will go. If you have been following the steps, you may have had the opportunity to sail different boats for each of your sailing classes.

When you charter a boat, you have a wonderful opportunity to spend time cooking and sleeping on board to get the real feel of her under way as well as comfort for living aboard. What many people do not understand is that unlike cars, where you can go to the dealership and take out each model for a test drive, when you are buying a boat, you do not get that option. Instead you write a check and sign a contract that states that you are committed to buying that boat, pending survey and sea trial. A dirty little secret in the industry is that on the sea trial, the surveyor may not even sail the boat, so you may not have any idea how she feels under sail. On a charter, you can put the boat to the test to see how it operates under power and under sail and what kind of sleeping comfort it offers.

More on what Lessons to Learn on a Bareboat Charter.

When making a float plan, calculate how much fuel and water you think you will consume. Be aware of your actual usage of fuel and water; think about what size tankage you will need or want on the boat. You will be responsible for provisioning and meal planning. Although it is different from actually living aboard, chartering will give you more real life experience to help develop the wish list for your cruising boat. What is the size of the refrigerator on the charter boat? Will it be large enough for you to provision for more than a week at a time?

During your charter you will also be monitoring the batteries, so make a note of the charging systems on board and how much you need to run the engine to keep the fridge cold and the batteries happy. This will call your attention to how many batteries you will need on the boat and what kind of charging sources you may want. The main point of the bareboat charter is your understanding of how to operate that boat and her systems.

Get to know a boat that is new to you.

As you go through your boat briefing with the representative from the charter base, you will be overwhelmed by the complexity of the boat and its systems. You may want to make a copy of our "Captains Checklist." We developed this list after operating many different vessels to help have a better grasp on key questions to ask during the boat briefing with the charter company. Many people sleep aboard the night before the charter actually begins, so use the checklist to locate the basic systems on the boat and see what you already understand. This will help you generate focused questions you can ask the base representative to review with you.

Check the rigging on the boat; make sure you understand how to work the windlass and anchoring system on the boat, practice deployment before you leave the dock.

Sail Captains Checklist

e/type/location: _____

[ ] **Anchors/Rode** [ ] Primary _____ [ ] Windlass _____

[ ] **Batteries** [ ] Location(s) [ ] Switches (locations and use)
       [ ] Capacity _____ [ ] Status
[ ] **Bilge Pumps** [ ] Auto Location(s) _____
[ ] Manual, Loc. _____ [ ] Handle located _____

[ ] **Deck Equipment** [ ] Fenders [ ] Dock lines [ ] Boat hook
[ ] Bucket [ ] Misc. cordage

[ ] **Electronics** [ ] Power On [ ] VHF Radio Test [ ] DSC: MMSI
[ ] GPS Model: _____ [ ] Autopilot Model: _____
[ ] Instruments : _____ [ ] Menu familiarization
[ ] **Navigation** [ ] Charts [ ] Chart work tools (Dividers, etc.)
[ ] Cruising Guides [ ] Pencils/etc.
[ ] **Electrical** [ ]Breaker Panel [ ] Inverter [ ] Battery Monitor
[ ]Generator Type/Location _____

[ ] **Engine** [ ] Filter(s) [ ] Oil [ ] Coolant [ ] Transmission
[ ] Stuff box [ ] Belts & Spares
[ ] **Fuel** [ ] Fill location(s) [ ] Tank location(s) [ ] Supply/Return Manifolds

[ ] **Linens** [ ] Bedding for all berths [ ] Towels for all staterooms and heads
[ ] **Provisions** [ ] Plan amount and type [ ] Properly stowed
[ ] Beverages [ ] Trash Bags, TP, etc.
[ ] **Refrigeration/Freezer:**[ ] Plumbing (Intake/outlet) _____
  [ ]Operating procedure [ ] Power requirements

[ ] **Rigging** [ ] Inspect Standing [ ] Inspect Running [ ] Inspect Blocks, etc.

[ ] **Safety Equipment** [ ] First Aid [ ] Flares, etc [ ] Fire Extinguishers
[ ] PFDs [ ] Signaling (whistle, horn) [ ] MOB gear [ ] Life raft [ ] Bug out Bag
[ ] Tools: locate and inventory [ ] Ships Papers

[ ] **Steering** [ ] Inspect steering cable(s) [ ] Inspect Rudder post stuff box
[ ] Emergency Tiller
[ ] **Thru hulls** [ ] Find locations & inspect [ ] Number found _____
[ ] Any of Concern _____

[ ] **Water: Fresh** [ ]Fill location(s) [ ] Tank location(s) [ ] Manifold
  [ ]Capacity _____ [ ] Status _____
[ ] **Water: Grey/Black** [ ] Pump out locations _____
[ ] Tank loc.(s) _____ [ ] Capacity _____
[ ]Status _____

The 10 things to test on your Bareboat Charter that will help you choose the right boat to buy.

1. Choose the size boat you feel comfortable handling.
Will your Bareboat Chartering experience lead to drama or have you paced yourselves so that your bareboat cruise feeds the dream? Drama example: We arrived in Tortola one time and on the day of our arrival, the upper half of the local paper had a picture of a sailboat up on the rocks right outside the base. Having worked for the base before, we were able to get some insight as to what had happened. Here's the story that we heard:

Ron & Linda, along with two other friends, chartered a 50' boat (15' larger than any boat they had ever operated) from a major charter company in the British Virgin Islands. Ron had the most sailing experience and was the designated captain of the boat. Captain Ron was very confident in his experience, but did not take into account the inexperience of the crew and his inexperience as a captain. Immediately after they cleared the rock jetty as they departed the base in Tortola, Captain Ron at the helm asked the crew to hoist the mainsail. As he was focused on watching the sail go up, he failed to keep the vessel into the wind. The main sail began to catch the wind and at the same time, the battens got caught in the lazy jack lines causing the sail to jam. He left the helm and ran forward, where the two other crew members were having trouble pulling as hard as they could on the halyard. He thought he could some how perform the task better, so he grabbed the line away from the crew and tried to haul the sail up. While they were all standing on the forward deck focused on the sail, the boat was sliding sideways and before they knew it, they crashed onto the rock jetty right next to the base. Lucky for them they were rescued, but the trip ended in short order and with around $15,000 damage. So what did they do wrong? How could you do better? Captain Ron was over confidant in what size boat he could handle and his ability to think ahead of the boat and coach the crew on what to do.

2. Practice controlling the boat under power then sail.

As Captain, you need to think way ahead of the crew and the boat; instead of hoisting the sail in a confined area, wait until you are in more open water. When you are at the helm, you need to focus on driving. The captain should be able to keep the boat into the wind, use the throttle to hold the boat on course, and NEVER abandon the helm.

When you are on a boat new to you, it would be prudent to wait to hoist the sails. Instead, practice under power first, noting the vessel's turning radius, how she reacts to the wind on her bow, and how well you can control her in reverse. Then set sail, practice a tack and control her through a jibe; you will have a better idea of how to handle the boat.

3. Communication skills: Give clear and concise instruction to your crew.

As you spend time on the water, think about the various captains with whom you have sailed. Think about how they directed the crew and consider the different approaches to command. Before you leave the dock, go over with the crew who will do which job and carefully explain how to perform each task. Explain what position to the wind the boat needs to be in order to hoist the sail and that it may foul in the lazy jacks. Test your crew's ability to figure out where the wind is coming from so that you can determine which crewmember may be better suited for which task. Delegate one crew to watch the battens. If the battens start to get caught, stop hauling up the sail, realize that you may need to lower the sail a little to free the sail and communicate this information to the crew. Have one person assigned to the halyard and one person assigned to ease off the main sheet so the sail can stay luffing while it is being hoisted.

4. Charter at least three different boats to make comparisons like monohull or catamaran.

Allow yourself this opportunity to try out different size boats, different layouts, or even a catamaran if you think you may like a cat instead of a monohull. Share the expenses with other like minded sailors, write up your own critique after your charter, and ask the crew what things they liked and didn't like about the boat. If you chartered a 35' to 38' for example, you may have felt very confident about how easy the boat was to handle, but if you shared that boat with a family of six, did the boat feel comfortable to everyone? If you tried out a catamaran, the living space probably felt very comfortable, but how well did she sail upwind, and how often did you have to motor to the anchorage? This is your time to begin your list of plus and minus factors that will help you make your decisions later of what size and type of boat you will want to own and cruise.

5. Observe other factors that affect comfort on board such as center cockpit versus aft cockpit.

The center cockpit monohull has a large aft stateroom; the trade off is comfort underway. With the center cockpit, you sit higher up, often above the lifelines, and as a result you feel more motion. For some people, a 45' center cockpit boat feels like only 30' of boat in front of you. When docking, that makes it seem easier to manage. Like Goldilocks, how are you really going to know what is just right for the two of you if you don't try out different boats? Challenge yourself to try a smaller 35' cruiser, then a 40' to 45' center cockpit boat, and then perhaps a 38' to 42' Catamaran. These different size and hull configurations will, at the least, give you a good sample of what other cruising couples are cruising on.

6. Sail in three different locations. Expose yourselves to different wind and sea conditions.

Each time you charter, you can gain valuable experience by sailing in different locations. This helps you add to your sailing resume and nurtures and feeds the cruising dream. Chartering in the BVI is a great first step because you only need line of sight navigation skills. Most nights can be spent on a mooring ball, and you are always a short dinghy ride from supplies or restaurants. This is why it is important to sail to different locations to experience different mooring, wind and sea conditions, as well as amenities nearby. Have fun looking over the different island choices and read the charter company guides to cruising the various areas while continuing to learn and grow your sailing skills.

7. Take turns as Captain on your Charter.

Bareboat chartering is also an ideal time to practice taking turns as captain. The very first time you sign all the paperwork for the charter, things change. You need to force yourself out of your comfort zone and learn to think through how to delegate what needs to be done. If you are always waiting for someone else to tell you what to do, you are not ready. Confidence builds slowly over time. You will be afraid at first but practice, practice, practice, and step up and be the captain. For your partner, this is also difficult, so step back and let mistakes happen. One of the hardest things to do as a teacher is to let your student screw up.

8. Practice your anchoring techniques.

This is a hot topic, as many sailing schools fall short on teaching proper technique. Also, by shear lack of experience, you will drag anchor at some point. We encourage couples to practice by anchoring out overnight. Here is a tip: when in doubt, let it out, scope that is, lots of scope, and then back the engine down at least 2/3 of regular motoring RPMs.

Of course, there is more to it. Things like: anchor tackle, holding ground, wind conditions at the time you anchor, predicted weather for the night, and choosing a good spot. You will also want to watch out for other boats in the anchorage, judging how close they are and whether all the boats will swing the same.

9. Plan out a week long cruise on your own and try to take into account what point of sail you will be on to reach your destination.

As you received your chart briefing from the charter company, did you start to think about what point of sail you would be on as you head from island to island? Did you start planning your route based on your crew comfort level for the various points of sail? If your crew is afraid of heeling the boat, you may want to think in terms of sailing on more of a reach. Start by choosing shorter distances, 12 to 15 miles, which can take three to four hours of sailing, more or less, depending on the point of sail, wind speed and sea conditions. If you plan twenty to thirty miles a day, you could be underway from dawn to dusk and never get a chance to enjoy the destination. Make sure you give yourself time to slow down your rat race pace, for the cruising lifestyle is a leisurely pace by design.

10. Consider the weather in your cruising plan so that you are safely at anchor or tied to the dock when bad weather passes.

When you charter in the BVI, do you look at the weather forecast for the week and take advantage of a wind shift? For example, with winds ESE, sail north up to Gorda Sound and then all the way up to Anegada. Then, as the wind shifts to the NNW, you head southwest to, say, Jost Van Dyke. This is a great time to think on the bigger picture instead of fighting each day beating up wind. Map out your route by which way the wind blows.

A tip for the Captain:

The captain needs to stay cool.

Yelling does not make things happen any faster.

Patience is active, it is concentrated strength.

The crew views the Captain's mood through a magnifying glass.
If the Captain is a bit nervous, the Crew is very nervous.
If the Captain is very nervous, the Crew is scared.
If the Captain is scared, the Crew is curled up on the cabin floor terrified.

This is one reason those old British Skippers are famous for their cool-as-ice demeanor even when all hell is breaking out around them. Among all the things a captain is responsible for, crew morale is one of the most important.

We have had situations with couples where the events that are happening are things we've experienced many times, and though we might not be comfortable, we're not concerned and just take the steps needed to get through it. Yet couples we are working with that have never experienced the situation are sometimes terrified. Good communication is the key here. We keep a running dialog going of what we are doing, why we are doing it, and what they can expect. This really helps calm them down so they can at least start breathing again.

It's all about the Captain's attitude!

A tip for the experienced crew:

Instead of jumping up and heading on deck to hoist the sail, ask the acting captain: "When would you like to raise the sails?" Then together discuss the plan: "Yes, I see that nice open spot ahead. I can get the sail ready and you let me know when to hoist." This allows the new captain a chance to think it through without being told what to do. If the boat isn't into the wind, do not even start to hoist; instead say, "I'm ready whenever you are"; wait, wait, then, if the helm still does not realize they are not into the wind, you might say, "You may need to come up into the wind a little more." Pretty soon they'll catch on.

New destinations to explore and learn. Go new places. Build your experience.

This is a good time to stop and reflect on the very first question we asked: where do you intend to cruise most? The answer may be coastal cruising to the Caribbean from the eastern shores of the U.S. Or some of you may have a plan to circumnavigate, in which case we still recommend laying a solid foundation by gaining experience cruising in the Caribbean. We want you to build on what you have learned so far. By now, you should have done a bareboat charter; most of you have cruised in the BVI.

Think about what you have learned so far. You should have had lots of experience picking up a mooring ball and planning your cruise based on which restaurant you wanted. Maybe on your charter vacation you selected "easy on the cook" provisioning and ate out for dinner most of the trip, but now, you want to try to practice planning for more meals aboard and being more selective about when to go out to eat.

We add this food for thought since most of us will have limited budgets or a fixed income while we are out cruising. Reality check: How often do you go out to eat at home and does that really work for your long-term financial goals? That's one reason we are big fans of the preview trip.

This is when you discover that Level 1 destinations such as the BVI are fabulous vacation spots, but as a cruiser, you will find them to be too expensive. For example, the mooring ball fees run about $30 per night, which adds up to $900 per month. That does not include water or shore power. It's just for the privilege of stopping in the anchorage.

Oh, but you thought you could anchor for free? Yes you can, but the BVI have very few of these spots where you can anchor for free, only lots of costly mooring balls.

Start thinking about limited resources. In the BVI, you can sail everyday to a different location and go to a store or restaurant. There are places to refill your water tanks, so if you have chartered there, you really have not had to budget for limited tankage or provisions.

Make plans for a week or ten days and factor in provisions such as water and fuel. Even if you were just thinking about cruising the East Coast of the United States along the Intracoastal Waterway (ICW) and possibly hopping over to the Bahamas, provisions can be an issue. There are places along the ICW where there is no cell phone coverage, no stores, and nobody around nearby. As you head over to the Bahamas, you will need to plan to go longer between re-provisioning and fuel stops. We want you to really think about how you use your water and limited resources. This will ultimately help you to know what kind of tankage and equipment choices you will be looking for on your cruising boat.

Travel Interlude. Examples of new destinations to explore.

Discovering new shores will motivate you to expand your knowledge and skills and make better decisions. You should expose yourselves to higher wind speeds and larger seas so you have had a chance to test your resolve. This section provides a view into different dream destinations, like Antigua, Guadeloupe, St. Vincent and the Grenadines, they await you, and are superb options for Level 2 & 3 charter locations.

Antigua anchorage

Antigua and Guadeloupe: The coastline of Antigua features many protected harbors, British naval history and a wall of coral reef that surrounds the island. A combination of hiking and snorkeling, along with great sailing, are some of the reasons this is one of our favorite islands. The island has good provisioning, which is one of the key factors to think about when considering living aboard. There are places to dock, anchor or pick up a mooring ball, so it offers a chance to practice all of these skills.

Try a one-way Charter and practice clearing in and out of Customs. Just to the south of Antigua lies Guadeloupe, so for those of you ready for more open water sailing, making the forty mile crossing to Deshaies is an excellent example of a typical short passage with your first exposure to real seas.

You will need to clear out of customs in Antigua and then find the customs officer in Deshaies to clear in. The Customs officer will appreciate if you learn a few words in French, even if you only know a few key words and phrases.

Explain you are trying to learn French, as this is seen as a sign of respect. You can often win over the customs official if you ask him about his country and what he recommends you visit on your stay. Little English is spoken in Deshaies. We recommend you get a reference book by Kathy Parsons *French for Cruisers*.

Guadeloupe is really two islands in the shape of a butterfly with the river Salee dividing the wings. The western side, known as Basse Terre (after its Capitol), is composed of lush tropical rainforest, waterfalls, sleeping volcanic mountains covered in lush green, plus acres of sugar cane, coffee and banana plantations. Fishing villages, as well as Jacque Cousteau's underwater marine park, dot the coast. To the south, between Guadeloupe and Dominica, lies a cluster of islands called Les Saintes. Your stop here should include time to snorkel off another island called Ilet a Cabrit, where you can see one of the best examples of golden brain coral in the Caribbean, as well as some interesting Moray eels.

To sum up a trip to Guadeloupe from Antigua, you'll experience open water sailing and then the charm of French villages along the coast. This is an opportunity to hike in the rainforest, bathe in one of the waterfalls, and sample the wine. In addition, you will get a chance to practice your French and deal with the customs officers in both English-speaking Antigua and French-speaking Guadeloupe. If you are not a seasoned traveler, this is a great chance to see how you handle visiting a foreign port and what it will be like cruising on your own. To enjoy the trip from Antigua to Guadeloupe, you should consider a one-way charter of at least two weeks.

St. Vincent & the Grenadines. St. Vincent and the smaller islands of the Grenadines together make up one country. Located in the southeastern corner of the Caribbean are islands that offer activities from mountain hiking to underwater snorkeling in coral gardens, full of colorful fish in the crystal clear waters. This is the path less traveled, so plan on spending one whole day to get there from North America.

St Vincent, the northern most and the largest of the islands features the movie set to "Pirates of the Caribbean." The water here is deep and clear and you can see the bottom in 30 feet of water. As a visiting yacht, you can drop anchor, then tie up stern to the very dock where Captain Jack Sparrow, aka Johnny Depp, stepped off his sinking boat.

Sailing south from Wallilabou Bay is one of our favorite island stops, **Bequia;** drop anchor in Admiralty Bay. Then shop for fresh fruit and veggies, which are sold daily in the market along with fresh baked bread. It is the only island where you can get your water tank filled and your laundry picked up from your boat in the anchorage.

Canouan is the next place to stop on your way south. Ashore, you'll find that the Moorings Charter Base and Tamarind Hotel has a beautiful beach right on the bay overlooking the yachts, with a big Tiki Hut Bar and restaurant, giving the ambiance of a Tahitian Village.

Anchored off the World's End Reef

The **Tobago Cays** are a grouping of five tiny islands inside a horseshoe shaped reef, which lies behind yet another reef. The reef is so large that it breaks the seas that come from across the Atlantic. Just on the other side of the reef there is not another piece of land until the continent of Africa. On **Union** Island, the southern most island in the Grenadines, is a local landmark called " Happy Island Bar." Its foundation is made up of conch shells, open sometimes, closed others. Smile, you're on island time!

Sailing conditions will include more open water sailing between the islands where cross setting currents, reefs and stronger breezes will challenge your navigation skills. Wind speeds average 15 – 25 knots in the late spring and early summer months or 20 - 30 knots in the winter season when the Christmas winds blow. A combination of picking up mooring balls and anchoring will give you basic skills practice next to real cruising boats and not just charterers. Limited access to replenish your water and fuel supplies, as well, will teach you how to monitor these precious resources. Allow yourself at least tens days to comfortably sail from St. Vincent to Union Island and return.

When you do return, on your own boat, you will already know the best places to stop and provision, and when not to pass up a place to refuel. You will have gained local knowledge from visiting the islands through the local charter companies, receiving the benefit of information they have on safety and security issues or if any really exist.

STEP 2 Checklist

1. You should both know and agree on what size boat you feel comfortable in handling.

2. You should both know and agree on monohull or catamaran.

3. You should both know and agree on what layout you would like to have on your boat.

4. You each can single-hand the boat and feel confident in controlling the boat under sail and under power.

5. You have good communication skills and give clear and concise instruction to your crew.

6. Together, you have sailed at least three different boats to make comparisons; for example, you have sailed different monohull brands like Island Packet or Catalina and sampled a catamaran.

7. You sailed in at least three different locations, exposing yourselves to different wind and sea conditions.

8. You each feel confident in the role as the responsible party for the boat and the safety of all the crew.

9. Together, you have planned and executed a week long cruise without crew and considered what point of sail you would be on to reach your destination.

10. Together, you considered the weather in your cruising plan, and were safely at anchor or tied to the dock before the bad weather arrived.

Resources

Charter Companies:

The Catamaran Company
www.catamarans.com

Conch Charters BVI
www.conchcharters.com

Dream Yacht Charters
www.dreamyachtcharter.com

Horizon Yacht Charters
www.horizonyachtcharters.com

The Moorings
www.moorings.com

Sailing Florida Charters
www.sailingflorida.com

Sunsail
www.sunsail.com

TMM Yacht Charters
www.tmm.com

Two Can Sail (Try a Catamaran, shared couples experience)
www.TwoCanSail.com

Step 3

Buy the right boat

STEP 3 Buy the right boat.

Are you crossing swords or are you on the same page?

How to choose and buy the right boat.
The factors to consider before you shop.

Five key points to consider before you shop: the budget, new or used boat, monohull or catamaran, your intended use (bluewater or coastal cruising), and the top ten yacht interior and exterior features and the compromises you may need to make. We have included an example of boat shopping questions and answers to help you focus on making a shopping spreadsheet of your own.

Examine your additional out of pocket costs such as taxes, insurance and other budget factors you should know about, to create your personal plan. Evaluate options, such as yacht financing or charter yacht ownership programs.

The budget: How much money do you plan to spend on the boat? What you want to spend will determine much of the remainder of your plans to buy a boat and go cruising. We want you to be realistic about your expectations as well. Most couples cruising today have selected 35 to 45 foot monohulls or 40 to 45 foot catamarans depending on their style and budget.

Here are some budget examples so you can plan accordingly:

Budget less than $100,000:
You will need to look for a boat around $50,000 and allow yourself a larger budget for repairs and upgrades (hold back about 50%). These boats can be found by taking your time and being really picky. It will take more time to find a boat in good enough condition to be worthy of added investment. Beware; some boats at this price range will cost more than your budget to turn into serviceable condition. If your survey comes back with more than 50 findings, walk away and keep on looking. We have worked with couples who have found the following boats in this price range: Island Packet 32, Endeavour 35, Catalina 36, Sabre 38, and a Pearson 424, to name a few.

Example: 1983 Sabre 38, nicely equipped $69,000

Example of $100,000 budget: Bill & Bonnie came to us with plans to sail to the Bahamas in the spring and summer. They had taken formal sailing classes and attended our seminar at the St. Petersburg Boat Show. After a long search, and viewing many not so nice boats, we finally came across this gem. The couple that owned her had used the boat exactly the way Bill & Bonnie planned on using the boat. She was equipped with an extra large refrigerator, watermaker, and was set up for extended stays at anchor. A perfect fit, but it took a lot of patience to find the right boat in their budget.

Budget of $150,000 to $225,000: In this price range, you will have many more choices and will be able to find newer used monohulls, as well as some older Catamarans. Examples of monohull boats in this range are the following: Island Packet's 38, 40 & 42; Catalina 42; Beneteau 43; Hunter 40 to 45's. Catamaran examples include: Leopard 39 & 40 and Fountain Pajot 36 & 42. There are many more examples, but these have been most popular. In these cases, the boats purchased in this price ranged from $115,000 to $160,000, allowing 30% for repairs and upgrades.

Example: 2002 Hunter 456, $169,000

Example of $225,000 Budget: Carrie and Collin were experienced boaters and had graduated from the ownership of several smaller boats from an O'Day 28 to a Catalina 42, both of which they sailed along the California coast. They wanted to spend time exploring the east coast of the U.S., as well as the out islands of the Bahamas. Carrie really wanted a boat that had a walk around berth and a shower stall separate from the head. This Hunter layout with a center cockpit and large aft deck fit the bill and was in the right budget. They have now been out cruising for more than three years, bouncing between south Florida and the Bahamas.

Budget of $250,000 to $400,000: This budget allows you to consider a new boat versus a used boat. With a new boat, you will need to allow more dollars for equipment. A used boat will often have buckets, boat hooks and many spare parts that the previous owner left on the boat and a new boat comes with nothing. See our basic recommended equipment list on page 164 of this book, which adds up to about $10,000 at the local marine supply store.

In this budget range, allow $75,000 to $120,000 for additional equipment after the purchase. An example of some of the boats that couples we have worked with chose include monohulls like the Catalina 445, Beneteau 46, Hunter 50, Jeanneau 45, and catamarans such as the Leopard 44, Dean 44, Manta 42 and Admiral 40.

Example: 2007 Dean 441 equipped for voyaging, $365,000

Example of $250,000 to $400,000 budget: Daisy and Daniel were dreaming of exploring the world via sailboat. They attended our Couples Cruising Seminar at the Miami Boat show, completed ASA basic keelboat sailing, coastal cruising and bareboat charter courses. Then they chartered on their own in the San Juan Islands, San Francisco Bay, British Virgin Islands and finally a trip to Thailand. They tried out both monohull and catamaran and found they really loved the added volume of the catamaran. This boat had just completed passage making with her previous owners and was ready to go. And now they have just completed the first phase of their voyage plans sailing from Florida to Grenada.

A budget of $500,000 and up gives you many new boat options, but you will want to get very specific as to what options actually come with the boat. One couple we worked with had a one million dollar budget. After adding up all the options on a new 50 foot catamaran, they found that the added options price came in with a price tag of $1.5 million. Some of our couples choose monohulls like the Outbound 46, Island Packet 485, Hylas 54, Passport 47 & 515 and the following catamarans: Antares 44, Knysna 480, Royal Cape Majestic 53 and the Privilege 4.5 & 49.

Example: 2014 Outbound 46 $575,000

Example of $500,000 plus budget: Eve and Edward attended our Couples Cruising seminar at the Annapolis Boat Show. Edward had sailed and raced for many years in his youth and Eve had just been introduced to sailing this year. Edward realized that his skills might be rusty and hired us to help get Eve more comfortable with handling the boat. Buying a new boat, Eve and Edward needed to also budget for buying all of the accessories that don't come with a new boat, from buckets and boat hooks to a Parasail spinnaker and drogue. They also ordered optional extras like radar and SSB with single side band and wisely planned on completing advanced training on this specialized gear. Included in their budget were additional funds for this added training.

A Typical Budget Plan

Here are some examples of how to plan for the boat purchase including the extra expenses.

1. Budget for the boat purchase $ 200,000
2. Budget 25% - 30% for extra expenses $ 60,000
3. Closing costs and USCG Documentation budget about 1% of purchase value.
4. Sales tax varies by state (anywhere from 5% to 13%); check with your state of residence .
5. Pre-purchase Survey $20 to $30 per foot,
Short (survey) haul out $250+,
Yard work and Repairs from the survey findings.
Make sure you understand the findings. This may lead you to re-negotiate price or pass.
6. Insurance - Compare the difference between Agreed value, Replacement and Actual cash value (2% of hull value is a good estimate for your annual coverage)
7. Ongoing maintenance (budget 2% per year)-
     bottom cleaning ($1-2 per foot per month)
8. Rigging & Sails- if they need repair or replacement.
          ($350+ for repair, $17000 for replacement)
9. Dockage & Fuel- Check rates and availability of slip.
             (Example: $12.50 per foot per month)
10. Dinghy - budget money for the other boat ($800 -10,000)
11. Added Safety Equipment like a life raft etc. ($3,600 and up)
12. Captain services: Delivery or Systems Training ($400 day +)
13. Unlimited Towing - For the first year of ownership est. $180 per year

Example: Budget for older boat $150,000
Nicely equipped with electronics, AC, Genset, VHF, SSB, canvas etc.
1990 Catalina 42 - $125,000

		Annual Insurance	$2500
Pre purchase survey	850	Monthly slip fee	525
Short Haul	250	Diver	75
Documentation	250		$3,100
7% Sales tax	8,750	Repairs	$3,350
	$135,100		
Used dinghy	2,350		
New Life raft	3,600		
5 days training	2,500		
	$143,550	GRAND TOTAL	$150,000

Old Boat versus New Boat

Older boats can have challenges yet can have some strong advantages. Our boat was 30 years old and overall in great shape. For this discussion we'll call "older" over 20 years.

Advantages of older boats:

1. Older boats often have better sailing hull forms for both performance and sea kindliness. Many of the new production boats have traded sailing quality and sea kindliness for interior volume, comfort at the dock, and shallow draft.

2. If you like real solid teak interiors, or other fine hardwoods, you almost have to get an older boat. These woods have become too rare and too expensive. The new boats all use either veneers or other less marine tolerant wood or just plastic.

3. Price. A brand new boat of same build quality and equipped the same as an older boat could cost over FIVE times the current value of the older boat.

4. If the hull, deck and basic structure is sound, then the value of the vessel is driven by the amount and age of equipment aboard. Most of your maintenance time will be with the systems as opposed to the basic structure. A used boat with new equipment can be a steal compared to a new boat.

5. Many of the boats built from the mid-60s to the early 80s had hulls that were overbuilt and very rugged. The business was fairly young and they didn't know just how much fiberglass they actually needed. Business was far more robust, so they could afford to spend the extra on making sure the hulls were very strong. Many modern production boats have taken the hull right to the minimum strength needed. This means they tend to flex much more than the older builds and this flexing leads to problems with the interior structure and rigging stability.

6. The old diesel engines were built very rugged, simple and extremely reliable. Most diesels, with rebuilds at the appropriate hours logged, could still be running another 30 years or more. The old diesels do not have components like turbo chargers or complicated computer controls that can cause the engine to be lost in case of electrical failures (e.g. lightning).

7. Boats thirty years old may be eligible for antique status which significantly reduces cost of annual registration fees.

Old Boat versus new boat.

Disadvantages of older boats:

1. Around 1990, boats began to be designed with spaces for things like air conditioning, watermakers, big TVs and big freezer systems. In an older boat, one needs to find places to squeeze these systems in which usually means giving up some storage somewhere.

2. Around 1990 to 1995, boats began to appear with the scoop stern to allow easy access to the water; this is a very nice feature rarely found in the older boats.

3. There are the possibilities of hidden issues in the structure and the method used to attach the rigging to the hull. One example of structural defects is delamination caused by a failure in the process used to wet out the fiberglass with resin. A good, intensive survey and rig inspection helps mitigate this concern, but cannot eliminate it. Picking an old boat with the right pedigree (i.e., quality built to start with) researching it and talking with current owners of the same boat helps significantly reduce this concern.

4. The old diesel engines are not as fuel efficient or environmentally friendly as the new ones. They are also larger and typically noisier with more vibration.

5. As boats get older than 8-10 years financing starts to become more restricted. The older the boat, the fewer banks there will be to choose from for financing and the less advantageous the rates.

6. Older boats have less interior volume for same overall length.

Monohull or catamaran trade offs are provided below to help you make your decision. A simplified comparison of monohulls and catamarans will give you enough of an outline; of course, the best way to decide is to sail them both.

Monohulls are more readily available, as they have been in production for many years. There are many different manufacturers that give you many designs and build factors as well as layout and sail plans.

Monohulls are also less expensive to buy and maintain. The various hull forms allow the vessel to move in sync with the seas.

With catamarans, you each get a hull. They are more stable, especially at anchor; two engines give you outstanding agility under power, as well as redundancy; and you have more interior volume, outstanding views from the main salon and fewer underwater thru-hulls.

Disadvantages: You have two hulls to maintain and two engines to maintain; upside down is more stable than right side up; there are more expensive dockage costs and limited availability of slips; and there is sharp "staccato" and less predictable motion at sea.

The question we get asked all the time is which is better. The answer is: it's a matter of personal taste. Just ask yourself whether you prefer dogs or cats as pets?

The TMM Fleet in Belize:
Lagoon 410, Fountain Pajot 36, Leopard 45, Leopard 46

Determine bluewater or coastal cruising; then choose the vessel's design to fit your style and budget.

In order to illustrate the differences between boats designed to circle the globe and those designed for coastal cruising, here are some factors to get you thinking about what the yacht designer had in mind for each purpose. Tankage: If you compare the length, beam and draft of different boats, they may seem very similar until you look at the tankage. There is more water and vastly more fuel capacity in vessels designed for offshore passages. Make certain to compare the fuel, water and waste tanks on your spreadsheet as you refine your shopping criteria.

An item that is rarely mentioned that we learned performing surveys, is that fiberglass is flexible. Fiberglass boats flex. A 36-foot to 40-foot fiberglass boat can flex up to 3 to 4 inches from bow to stern in normal operation in seas. They will also flex torsionally; that is, they will twist about their fore/aft centerline. The less expensive the boat, the lighter built the boat will be in order to meet the cost points. The lighter boats tend to flex much more than heavier boats built for ocean passages. This does not mean light boats are unsafe. It means when you finish a tough crossing, you're much more likely to have leaking hatches and side ports, doors that won't close, and systems that have worked loose inside.

When buying a boat, you will need to consider what factors are most important to you and how you want to use the boat. Decide whether you plan to circumnavigate offshore in bluewater, or just go coastal cruising to the Caribbean. Be realistic with yourselves, since there are many more choices in coastal cruisers versus true bluewater designed boats.

Example Coastal Racer/Cruiser: *Our C&C 38R (1979) was a great boat and really fun to sail. In fact, we won a lot of races with her. Consider her a Porsche. Each year, we'd race her from Clearwater to Key West (220 nautical miles) and before we'd leave, we'd make sure none of the ports or hatches leaked. Since she was built to be light and fast, she flexed, so by the time we got home all of the leaks had opened up again. That's life with a hard-driven race boat.*

Example Bluewater/ Offshore Cruiser: *In contrast to the C&C story above, our Skye 51 was designed as a performance (circa 1981) ocean cruiser. The Skye had six bulkheads that ran the full height and beam of the boat, compared to one on the C&C. She had an over-built hull thickness reinforced with six large stringers that ran the full fore to aft on either side, and had a massive matrix of fiberglass over the keel section. Even after a crossing in a full gale (38kn sustained with gusts in the 50s) and seas 15-20 feet, there were no leaks.*

Example Coastal boat on bluewater passage: *We knew of a new 44' Deck Salon version of a low cost production boat that in its first year, did a trip from Florida to Mexico (1000 nautical miles round trip). Winds reached 25 knots with seas to match. By the time the boat returned to Florida, the wind instruments had been tossed off the mast head from a violent pitching and rolling movement the boat developed. None of the doors to the staterooms would close properly, nor would the companionway door slide closed, due to the twisting and flexing she experienced in seas, that by ocean standards, were moderate at most. Her owner noted that he would stick to coastal cruising from now on, which was really his intended use in the first place.*

Consider which is most important to you, price or quality.

Determine whether you want the top of the line boat, which might last forever, or a less expensive version that you'll have to replace when it wears out. Quality is very important, but ultimately, it is price that is the decision factor for most of us. There is an even broader range of build and equipment options for boats than there is for cars, so this is obviously a very big factor in determining the price range.

If you're buying a new boat and it is the least expensive by far for a boat of its size, there is a reason. There is no magic out there. The builder has to use the lowest cost parts for every process at every stage in order to get to that price point.

This is not right or wrong! These boats are still safe for most usages. It is a question of personal taste, budget, and what kind of motion at sea you are comfortable with. There will be a difference in ease of maintenance and how long the parts will last. The least expensive boats will use the least expensive parts which often means they are harder to maintain (example: engine sea strainers and fuel filters), and these parts will wear out sooner or break easier under stressful conditions.

It may seem that if you are spending $300,000 or more on a new boat, a high level of quality is expected. However, if most of the other boats for sale of the same size as the boat you purchased for $300,000 sell for $500,000 to $1,000,000, then there must be a reason the $300,000 boat is so much less expensive.

Example of price versus quality:
One day, we were on our boat at our slip doing general maintenance. Our slip neighbor, who had recently spent $300,000 buying his first sailboat (the least expensive 45' on the market), was working on his engine sea strainer. He started swearing at the strainer as being a "cheap piece of $%^&" and popped up exclaiming that he "spent enough money on this boat, they ought to have used decent quality parts." If you want decent quality parts, you'll need to spend the money to buy a high quality boat because there is a difference. If your intended use is day sailing a couple weekends a month on bays or lakes, the difference in the parts may mean nothing. If your intended use is a circumnavigation, it is everything.

Offshore style U shape   Charter style linear galley

Monohull galley trade offs:

The shape and location of the galley is different for bluewater sailing and cooking underway. On a monohull, the galley will be smaller, with the ability to limit the cook from flying around. The size and style of the refrigerator is also different; example, a front-loading 2.5 cu ft. is designed for coastal hops, whereas a larger 6.0 cu ft. refrigerator is designed for longer voyages. The top loading style allows the cold air to stay in the refrigerator so that each time you open the top to get something out, it does not cause the motor to kick on. Therefore, it uses less power. There is nothing wrong with the smaller front-opening refrigerator, but it helps illustrate some of these additional factors we want you to consider on both monohulls and catamarans.

Island style aft berth   Pullman at the center of motion

Monohull berth configurations:

In a monohull, a V-berth all the way forward is great at anchor for good ventilation, but in a seaway, you will find yourself lifted in flight while underway. When the head is all the way forward and the berth is offset near the mast and the center of motion of the boat, you will have better comfort underway. A coastal cruiser may have a large centerline queen or even king size berth, which are spectacular for sleeping aboard at anchor or the dock. But when you are underway, you will fly off the bed as the boat moves.

Once you determine your intended use for the boat, you should now have more information to choose which boats are truly designed for bluewater ocean voyaging versus coastal cruising. And now that you know a little more about factors to consider in your shopping process, you will understand that every boat is a compromise and you can choose what is most important to you as a couple.

Catamaran trade offs for couples. Catamarans come in lots of different layout versions. It is not as clear cut which one to choose from, so we have made a list of some of the key factors you can look at to help you decide what your compromises will be for you as a couple.

Helm located in the cockpit is prefered.

1. Helm location: Visibility from the helm is important. For couples, we highly recommend that the helm station be inside the cockpit. Check to see if you can see all four corners of the vessel for docking with only two people.

2. Galley styles: A galley down is often chosen for voyaging, as it is the most secure for cooking underway. A compromise design would be the galley up, in a U shape, secure but still able to socialize with the cook. The least desirable is the aft facing, long straight galley with nothing to hold on to. Check the size and style of the refrigeration and try to picture provisions for two weeks.

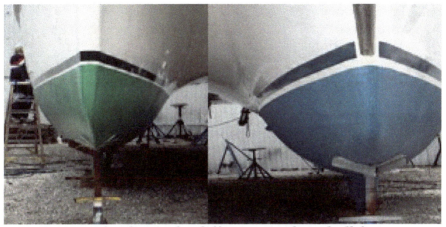
You can clearly see the difference in these hull forms.

3. Hull forms: Narrower hulls with a long waterline provide a more sea kindly motion. Wider hull designs are to maximize volume below deck. Look at the height of the bridge deck; will the waves slap and pound under the salon sole underway in seas? If the transom is open to allow easy access for swimming, then it leaves the aft section of the cockpit open. This could leave you standing in water in the cockpit if a wave breaks over the stern.

4. Engine horsepower: The boat needs to have enough horsepower (HP) to account for the windage. A forty-foot catamaran should have at least two 40 HP engines to account for the windage. Check the rudder position; one aft of the prop will give you better steerage for maneuvering at the dock. Consider the engine access and location for maintenance. How cramped is the space for you to be able to change the oil or a fuel filter? Think about what will it be like in a seaway.

This is a good example of offshore dinghy storage.

5. Transom and dinghy stowage: Look to see how secure the dinghy will be underway. In protected waters, we have often had the dinghy swaying madly, even when secured with six lines in an attempt to better secure it for conditions. Check to see how high off the water the davits are and if the dinghy can be properly secured. For voyaging, having the ability for the dinghy to be set in a cradle and locked down, as pictured above, would be preferred.

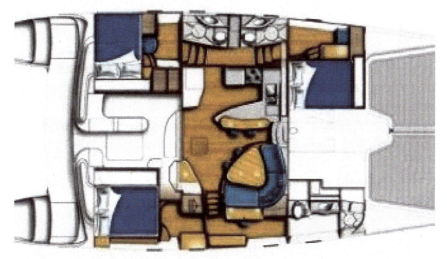

Pictured above is an example of a three-cabin layout.

6. Layout: Four-stateroom, four head charter version or three-stateroom three head owner's version? Be flexible, you may find everything you want in a four cabin, two head boat, even if you have been focused on finding an owner's version, so keep an open mind. On catamarans, the owner's version layout will feature the master stateroom aft. This layout allows for a large head and shower stall and office or storage space but does not take into consideration the ventilation to the aft berth. The deck hatch for this aft cabin layout is often blocked by the cabin top, which limits the amount of airflow below while at anchor. When considering catamarans, make sure there is enough airflow below for sleeping comfort. Try to visualize the extra cabin as an office or the machine shop, maybe convert the extra head into the wet locker or laundry. We know of one couple that converted the starboard forward cabin into the office and the portside aft cabin into the workshop. Just remember to balance the weight.

7. Sailing features: Check to see how swept back the spreaders are; now imagine yourself sailing downwind. Can you let the boom out without hitting the spreaders? Check for a set up for a spinnaker or whether you can sail downwind with the Genoa. It is good to have a balance between the Genoa and main. Imagine going through a gibe; there should be enough winches for you to have both the main and the jib on a winch. The more winches, the better. The sail controls should be led in such a way that the two of you can tack and gibe easily. Check out the location of all the winches; you should be able to lead the furling gear to a winch.

8. Weight to Length and Sail Area: A heavier boat will be slower but have better motion at sea, and if she has enough sail area, she will still carry you at a comfortable pace. If you are more performance oriented, be ready to sacrifice interior volume for speed. We have also found that catamarans with a 50% beam to length ratio or less have a better motion comfort factor, so, for example, a 42' boat with a 21' beam has more sea kindly motion than say a 36' boat with a 21' beam.

9. Anchor set up: Does the anchor drop underneath the centerline of the boat or does the anchor deploy on the bow from the crossbeam? If the anchor deploys from the center of the vessel as the wind blows the boat off, you will have to manage the boat so that the anchor chain does not scrape the hulls under the waterline. Whereas, when the anchor is off the bow, the boat will blow away from the chain and not over the chain. This is just one more way of observing the subtle differences with catamaran designs.

It's best when the anchor deploys from the bow.

10. Tankage: Again compare fuel and water capacity. Boats designed for charter fleets will be light on tankage because they are never far from supplies. If you want to go on longer trips, consider a boat with a larger fuel capacity, perhaps a set up with two fuel tanks. Water tankage is not as crucial, as you can install a watermaker and have an unlimited supply of water.

In Summary
When picking out these key factors, make your own personal list of comparisons between the boats you like and then decide where compromises are needed. There are few truly bad boat designs, and for the most part, all of the modern builders are crafting safe boats. The issues at hand are finding the boat that suits your tastes and fits your intended use.

Top 10 - Interior features to consider.

The following features are applicable to both monohull and multihull to provide live aboard qualities similar to your land home.

1. Bed Configuration: Decide what type of bed configuration suits you: a v-berth forward (best air flow at anchor); a Pullman berth near the center of motion on the boat (provides the best comfort underway); or maybe a large island queen berth aft (closest berth style to your land home bed).

2. Heads: How many heads do you want? And do you need a separate shower stall or is a "wet head", which you'll have to clean after each shower, ok?

3. Heating and Cooling: In order to have home comfort while living at anchor, you will need DC powered 12-volt fans in every stateroom, main salon and galley. You may want reverse cycle heat and air-conditioning installed so that, at the very least, you have climate control when connected to shore power. This will be a must if you plan to spend a summer at the dock in Florida. A very nice feature is the ability to run the air-conditioning or heat at anchor from a generator, if your budget allows.

4. Galley: You will want a galley that is secure for cooking underway with a gimbaled LPG (liquid propane gas) stove and oven for ease of cooking aboard. We prefer LPG because it is available everywhere.

5. Large refrigeration and freezer: You will need sufficient refrigerator and freezer space that allows you to eat fresh food and carry enough items for a trip through the out islands of the Bahamas, where provisions are few and far between.

6. Batteries – lots of batteries: Make sure you have a bare minimum of 400 Amp hours and preferably as much as 800 to 900 Amp hours with multiple charging sources.

7. Inverter/charger with a battery monitoring system: An inverter/charger with battery monitoring system is needed so that you can see not only how much power each item draws, but how charging sources are operating. The inverter, combined with a large battery bank, allows the comforts of running your single cup coffee brewer or crock-pot while charging your iPhone.

8. Storage: You'll need lots of spaces and cubbies to store the wine, dry goods, as well as maintenance spares, engine hoses and oil filters etc.

9. Tankage: You want the largest fuel tank available for the boat size on the market. You can always get a watermaker to replenish your water, but a larger fuel tank allows you more choices to motor if you need to make way against the wind.

10. Ventilation: You'll want to have plenty of hatches and opening port lights that allow for good airflow through the boat when you are at anchor.

Top 10- Exterior features to consider.

The following features also apply to both monohull and catamaran. The features that each specific boat has may help you compare why one boat that appears to be exactly the same is priced differently.

1. Shelter from the weather, wind and waves. You will want both a dodger that protects the companionway and a bimini structure to shelter you from both sun and rain. If you want to bask in the sun, just lay out on deck. The best shelter, if the budget allows, would be a complete enclosure. An enclosure expands your living space to the cockpit, where you will enjoy more than just sunsets with new friends. If the boat does not have an enclosure, consider budgeting to add it.

2. Sail features: A traditional main sail that flakes on the boom is best in all wind speeds; adding a "Mack Pack" stack pack allows you to drop the main right into the patented sail cover and lazy jack system. Alternatively, you may want an in -boom furling main, which allows for heavier cloth and full battens on the main that can be reefed, keeping its shape in even heavy air conditions. You may prefer the in-mast style of main sail. Keep in mind, this sail can never be constructed of heavy cloth, as it needs to fit inside the mast. The important thing to remember with in-mast furling style main is to reef early before the weather hits you.

3. Sail controls should lead to the cockpit so that you do not need to go on deck to shorten the sail. In addition, the furling gear should also be lead to the cockpit and preferably to a winch. If possible, the drum of the Genoa furling gear should be open so that if the line jams, it can be cleared without having to disassemble it with small tools while the sail is flogging in the wind.

4. An anchor system that can be operated by anyone under 100 pounds, preferably with a remote control that allows both up and down motion of the windlass.

5. A swim ladder that can be accessed from the water. If someone goes overboard, consider how easy it will be for that person to get back on the boat from the water.

6. A clean deck and side decks that you can walk around with handholds in appropriate spots. Lifelines should be taller than your knees, the higher the better, so there is less chance of a man overboard situation.

7. Storage: A place to store dock lines and fenders that you can easily access when you are coming into a marina.

8. Safety equipment: Check the vessel's added safety gear like liferaft or Emergency Position Radio Indicator Beacon (E.P.R.I.B.) Check the dates on the flares and fire extinguishers; in addition, check the condition of the life jackets and throwable devices like Life Sling or MOB equipment.

9. Dinghy storage: If the vessel has a davit structure, it needs to be strong enough to also withstand shock loading of the weight on the stern while underway. If the davits weigh the stern down, then you may need to add more weight to the bow to balance the load lines. You will want lifting tackle for the outboard, as well. If there are no davits, then you will want the boat to have an electric winch, so that you can hoist the dinghy onto the foredeck for open water sailing.

10. Single lever throttle control easily in reach for operation.

Top 10 - Electronics are as follows:

1. VHF (Very High Frequency) Radio connected to a GPS, registered with MMSI# entered into radio and a remote command mic at the helm.

2. VHF masthead antenna (at a minimum) that splits the reception of VHF and Automatic Identification System (AIS) broadcasts and then displays the AIS data on the chartplotter. The ability to receive AIS transmissions (automatic identification system) that all commercial ships must broadcast will take the blinders off. If you can receive this data, you can see the name of the ship, its course and speed and whether you are on a collision course.

3. Independent GPS antenna that can feed data to the radio and will back up the built in GPS in the chartplotter. This will add redundancy to your system should you loose your plotter.

4. A chartplotter that displays AIS targets as well as position and charts which can be updated as new charts are issued.

5. Autopilot with an independent control head that is not just run through your chartplotter. The autopilot system is one of the most critical systems. The autopilot is what enables two people to manage all aspects of running the vessel. The preferred type of autopilot would be a hydraulic ram pilot that connects directly to the rudderpost, as opposed to the one that connects via plastic parts around the wheel.

6. Depth sounder: If you have a catamaran, consider spending a few dollars more and placing a depth sounder in each hull. With the hulls as much as 24 feet apart, there can be a considerable difference in depth between the two hulls. In the narrow channels and the shallow waters of Florida, the ICW and the Bahamas, the second sounder would be worth the added investment.

7. A through-the-water knot meter and water temperature sensor. This combo is a good choice. If you plan to sail to the Bahamas, you will cross the Gulfstream, and knowing your speed through water (STW), as well as the water temperature, can aide in your navigation.

8. A wind speed and direction indicator that displays this data to an instrument located or installed near the helm.

9. A Single Side Band (SSB) Radio allows you to broadcast and receive long distance communications. As you head further away from civilization this becomes your primary source for voice and email communications with family and friends. By adding a Pactor modem, you can have email at sea. You will need time to learn how to use this tool. It is not plug and play, so allow time in your plan to test before you head off to distant shores.

10. Radar: If you have enough in the budget, we suggest you install radar. Receiving your own local radar is useful not only for collision avoidance but for seeing weather at a considerable distance and the sea state outside of an anchorage. Radar is also a powerful navigation tool, showing "what is" as opposed to the chart plotter's "what may be". Radar is not an intuitive tool; you will need to get additional training to understand and interpret the information properly.

This is a sample of the boat-buying questionnaire that we send to our clients. This is a paraphrase of an actual questionnaire from a couple.

What kind of sailing will be done? Depending on season, weather, etc. and as we get more comfortable with the boat: Fairly extensive sailing for 6 months, then home for 6 months, then sailing again, etc.

Where will sailing be done? Coastal (eventually Eastern US & Canada, Gulf Coast, Bahamas & Caribbean passages)

How much time consecutively underway? 2-3 days max. Possibly more if required, but not normal

When not underway, do you plan to be at anchor or on a mooring or at a slip? Anchored as much as possible

How long do you anticipate owning & using the boat?
3-4 years of "major" sailing time, likely keep boat 3-4 years after that

What is your price range to buy the boat?
Up to $150,000 in really good shape. $190,000 total available to acquire & upgrade a boat if necessary

Type of boat sought? Sloop rigged sailboat/monohull

Size of boat sought? 40-44 feet with size based on first mates' ability, also future cruising costs and comfort.

Particular items of interest desired in the boat?
Would like an anchor windlass that powers both Up & Down
Electric head with manual backup, holding tank and macerator
Easy access & maneuverability in cockpit while at helm with lines leading to the cockpit, Max draft 5 foot with 2 Cabins

Comments
Captain & crew are able to perform maintenance & upgrades very much on their own, but life in a boatyard is not the retirement dream.

This couple shopped for about six months before finding the right boat.

Boat shopping should be fun and should not be rushed. There is much to consider when choosing a boat and it is a very personal decision.

We ask you a lot of questions about where you intend to sail and how you are planning to use the boat and what your budget plan is for both the boat and the cruising kitty. This is how we help you develop your own spreadsheet and wade through the multiplicity of boats on the market to narrow down your selection.

Insurance and financing your dream boat.

Shop for insurance. In the good old days of the 1980's, people would sell their home to pay for the boat, sailing with the simplest systems and putting it all at risk, going uninsured. Today, the significant investment you are making in your cruising boat calls for the strong recommendation of insurance. You should take time to consider the different insurance policies as you would in a home purchase. The bank requires certain insurance to cover the investment and you should too.

Meet with an insurance agent that brokers a variety of companies, so that you can comparison shop. Only get insurance for what you are doing with the boat right now. If you are planning on coastal cruising first, then start with that cruising area.

You may also find, as you start to shop for insurance, that you may need to prove you are capable to sail the boat of the size you are planning to buy. Every year we see more couples buying a 50 foot yacht as their first boat. Finally, the insurance companies are stepping in and are starting to require a captain for the boat until the couple gains sufficient experience.

Make sure you know where you plan on docking the boat as this will affect your policy. You may be expected to have a hurricane plan even if you plan on keeping the boat up north.

Ask your agent to carefully explain the difference between "Agreed value" and "Actual cash value" so that if one policy seems a lot less than the other, you may understand why the difference in price. You need to know what kind of deductible the policy has and what they cover if you take a lightning strike or get dismasted. Both of these events have happened to us, and, in the case of the lightning strike, we have actually been struck twice. These incidents could have been complete financial disasters for us had we not had excellent coverage. If one policy quote seems a lot cheaper than another, it probably doesn't cover the same things.

You will need to provide to the insurance company; the survey report for the valuation of the vessel, your sailing resume, where you plan on keeping the boat and where you plan on cruising. Be prepared to share this information with your insurance broker. Hopefully, these points will give you the basic questions to ask your insurance agent/broker, who will help you determine what policy needs you have, and of course, give professional advise on what is best for you.

Consider your financial options. After you have considered these five factors: budget, new or used, monohull or catamaran, bluewater or coastal, and the list of features that fits your needs, you want to consider getting pre-approval for a loan, even if you plan on paying cash. If you plan on selling your home to raise funds for your boat, you may want to apply for a boat loan while you still own a home and have a job. These factors are important to the bank and may give you a larger budget with which to shop. The lending rules are different; if you tell the bank you plan to make the boat your home, then it is next to impossible to get a loan. After all, you are telling them you plan to sail away with the collateral. When you start shopping, you may find that you can't find a boat you like within your initial budget. By having financing in place, you may be able to get a much nicer boat with less additional equipment to install after the purchase. In addition, the sales tax may be added to your financing, so make sure to check with your lender. After you buy the boat, you will have more time to transition out of your land home and onto the boat. When you sell your home, you can pay off the note, and have your cruising boat fully equipped and ready to set sail.

In following our first two steps, you may have discovered that fulltime liveaboard cruising may be years away. You may want to consider using one of the many charter purchase options. This would allow you to buy a boat sooner rather than later, giving you time to gain more experience while you are still working. Check out the various charter company's ownership programs, to determine if this is an option for you.

What you need to know about the purchase process.

Now that you've become familiar with various boat styles, systems, and levels of comfort that are right for you, it is time to go boat shopping and make the best selection for your needs. The purchase process will cover: tips on how to go boat shopping; dealing with boat brokers; how and why you should select a broker to assist you in the process; making a spread sheet to compare vessels; visiting the boats in person to compare actual condition of the available boats; making an offer and choosing a surveyor to evaluate the vessel. Other factors you need to have in place will be: a name for the boat; insurance for your present needs; a place to keep her; a plan for addressing repairs or upgrades; and ongoing maintenance.

Why you should choose a broker and surveyor.

When you go to buy a boat, the likelihood is that you'll deal with a broker. Just as in real estate, there are two types of brokers: one that represents the seller, and one that represents the buyer. The listing yacht broker's responsibility is to sell the boat. The buyer's broker's job is to act as the buyer's representative (middleman) in negotiating the sale. Regardless of whether you are dealing directly with the listing yacht broker or the buyer's broker, you want the best outcome possible. Ask the broker about his or her boating experience and see if they really understand how you want to use the boat. Keep talking to different brokers until you find someone who understands your needs. They should help you compare the various models that you have looked at, the different equipment and condition, etc. When you have a good match you will know that you found the right broker.

If you walk into a broker's office and say "I want to buy that boat," he will sell you that boat, regardless whether it is right for you or not. This isn't because he's a bad person or lacking integrity. His integrity and financial responsibility is to the seller and to sell that boat, not be your consultant. The good brokers will go home upset and worried about you, but there is nothing they can do without breaking their contract with the seller. If, instead, you walk into the same good broker's office and say, "I would like to buy a boat. Can you help me find one that fits my needs and intended use?", you'll then have a valuable ally who will assist in your search.

A buyer's broker is different, in that they represent buyers. They are on your side of the table, helping you search, find, negotiate, and move through the closing process to buy the boat. A buyer's broker can provide value-added services that are paid for entirely by the seller under the standard yacht brokerage commission structure. There are no additional costs for a buyer to work with a buyer's broker. The broker splits the commission that the seller pays with the listing broker.

Find a dedicated buyer's broker, one that you like, trust and feel you can develop a rapport with, and commit to working with them only. When your buyer's broker calls those other brokers on the Yacht World listings, the listing brokers will know this is a serious deal and pay attention. Often, there is information about the boat or deal that is awkward or undiplomatic to discuss with the buyer, but will be discussed with a Buyer's Broker.

Select a surveyor who has experience in the type of boat you are buying.

Now that you have made a decision to buy a specific boat, you need to have it surveyed. A boat survey is similar to a home inspection prior to sale and is an essential step in making sure your investment is seaworthy. The surveyor should do a thorough inspection and provide a written report, which is a legal statement of the condition of the vessel and the status of the equipment, as well as the valuation of the boat as a whole. A good survey may be used for further negotiations in the purchase process.

Consider shopping for a surveyor while shopping for your boat. This will allow you to have someone you trust lined up and ready when you put in an offer. All too often, we get calls that sound like this: "I need a survey tomorrow, what's your price?" We almost never take these jobs. It's clear the buyer doesn't understand how important a survey is, what a survey can do for them, and the difference in value between different surveyors and what they offer.

Select a surveyor who has experience with the type of boat you are looking at and, preferably, one who has actual experience cruising! The two most recognized international organizations are the Society of Accredited Marine Surveyors (SAMS) and the National Association of Marine Surveyors (NAMS). It is not uncommon for Insurance and Mortgage companies to require a SAMS or NAMS surveyor. A surveyor should not survey a vessel that is outside their experience. We know some outstanding, highly skilled surveyors who specialize in large sports fish and cigarette type vessels who should not survey cruising sailboats. Your best choice would be a surveyor who focuses on cruising sailboats.

Do not expect your surveyor to tell you you've picked the wrong boat type. The surveyor's job is to tell you the condition of that specific boat, not to be a consultant. Only if the difference between boat type and intended use is dramatic will the surveyor (versus a consultant) say anything to you about the boat you are choosing to purchase (example: if you're looking at a Macgregor 22 and planning to do a high latitude circumnavigation).

When you receive the written survey report, read it carefully and discuss any questions you have with the surveyor. Ask questions if you do not understand the terms used in the report. Review the findings with your broker and see if there is cause to renegotiate the deal, or maybe, reject that boat and keep looking. There have been a few times that we came to survey a boat and it was in such a pitiful state that we called off the survey. When a boat is in "Poor condition" the liability of trying to "find and report" everything wrong with the boat can outweigh the money earned by producing a survey. This brings us also to what you should expect from the survey. Finding a surveyor that will test each system on the boat and sail the boat on a sea trial is great. However, time at sea is a factor in being able to test and evaluate every system. A surveyor may not be able to find everything wrong with the boat in a short period of time on board. Many systems need hours of use to determine if they are truly functioning properly.

Things that are reported in the "Findings and Recommendations" can give you insight into what else may be wrong with the vessel. If there are a large number of findings, you should consider it a big red flag that even more will be uncovered after you buy the boat.

The Boat Purchasing Process.

Now that you have finally found the boat in the best condition with the most features that match your criteria, it is time to make an offer! Your broker (hopefully you have a "buyer's broker" on your side of the table) should already have a form to use and help you decide how much to offer. Unlike many things we buy, you can offer less than asking price. Many sellers start with a high price figuring they can always come down. If you are like many people, you are not used to negotiating. Your broker can assist you with this aspect of the purchase. Negotiation is certainly expected in boat transactions in the United States. Occasionally, a vessel will be listed with a very reasonable price to start with, and these sell very quickly.

Before making the offer, consider the current status of the market for boats. If you have been out there shopping and you know that you found the cleanest boat with the best equipment, you may need to just offer the asking price. You will still be able to negotiate or reject the boat, pending the survey and sea trial. As part of the initial offer process, your broker can have an informal discussion with the listing broker to understand how flexible the seller may be. Your broker will also research the market, using online tools available only to brokers and surveyors to determine what comparable boats have sold for and what they feel a fair price would be. In addition, they will have discussions with you to determine an initial offer price.

Your broker then creates a formal offer contract that includes the offer price, has you sign the contract and lists the milestone dates that the seller and buyer must meet. These dates are:
1. Seller: date by which the seller must respond to the offer, either with acceptance, or a counter offer. If this date is not met the offer is rescinded.

2. Buyer: date by which the survey and any other inspections (like an engine survey) will be completed and the vessel either accepted (with a signed form) or rejected.
3. Buyer: date by which closing will be completed and title transferred.

The negotiation is often done by email. Once a price is agreed upon, a deposit check of 10% of the price is provided by the buyer and held in escrow by your buyer's broker in their escrow account. If the vessel is rejected from the survey or sea trial, the deposit is refunded. If the buyer just "walks away" from the deal without cause, the deposit is forfeited.

After the offer has been accepted, you will need to schedule the survey, short haul and sea trial. We have discussed choosing a surveyor and what the survey may or may not find. One more aspect of the survey to consider is inspecting the boat out of the water, or the "out of water" survey. This is usually done by bringing the boat to a yard with the proper size lift to haul her out. The boat gets hauled into the slings, which allows you to examine the underwater machinery as she sits in the slings. This is called a short haul. We usually recommend that the buyer request the yard wash the bottom with a fresh water pressure wash. This allows the hull to dry more quickly, and gives the surveyor the best opportunity to examine the hull.

This will also be your opportunity to see the bottom of the boat and examine the keel, rudder, propeller and the condition of the hull and bottom paint. As the surveyor is going through the boat, you can ask questions about what is of concern and/or what is "normal wear and tear." While you are at the yard, ask to speak to the yard manager and get an estimate on a bottom paint job, or if something else is uncovered, ask for a quote to fix it. This will help you put dollar value on potential repairs, which can be used to negotiate the price with the seller.

The seller will need to captain the boat or provide a captain to take her to the yard for haul out and to operate the boat on the sea trial. The sea trial should include operation of the boat under both power and sail. If you are buying a sailboat, you should ask that the sea trial include sailing. This may not be possible if the weather conditions do not allow, but in most cases, you should be able to have a short sail and get a visual view of all of the sails that are included with the purchase. Test sail close hauled on port and starboard tack, feel the tension on the rigging. Check to see how easily the jib sheet cars move and the winches and lines operate. Take note if the binnacle compass matches the chartplotter. Does the binnacle match the auto pilot control head? Test the autopilot and determine if it holds course.

In addition, test the engine for operation at maximum rpm's along with a test backing down in reverse. The surveyor will check the amount of vibration in the engine mounts, which could indicate a shaft misalignment. These things will help to determine if the prop and shaft are tuned properly.

If there is a generator, have it started and run a load to test for operation. If the boat comes with a dinghy and outboard, there may not be an opportunity to test these, but ask when the outboard was last used and how it was stored. If it was not stored properly, it could take a visit to the outboard mechanic to get it back in operating order. When the survey is complete, the report should be reviewed with the Surveyor. It is not uncommon for issues to be found that the seller was unaware of; consequently, the price can be renegotiated based on the findings. If there are no issues or if a new price is negotiated (with the offer contract updated and re-signed by both parties), then the closing date is scheduled within the time frame originally noted. If there are issues and agreement is not reached, then the deal is off and the deposit refunded.

Request the survey report to be emailed to you in an electronic format that you can use to send out for insurance or financing. Once you get the report and you have agreed on the price and other terms, you will need to sign an "Acceptance of Vessel" (AOV). Once the buyer has signed the AOV, the deal moves to closing. The buying side brokerage handles the escrow, closing paperwork, and funds transfer.

If it's not in writing, it doesn't count. Verbal commitments amongst people of good faith may be fine, but even people of good faith forget, or get misquoted. There is an adage that customers hear what they want to hear, not necessarily what you said, and it is often true. This can cause very expensive problems when buying a $200,000 (or much more) boat. With advanced communications technologies, there is no reason not to put it in writing. If the dealer/salesperson makes a verbal commitment on something, ask them to send an email confirming that or send them one saying, "We heard you commit to _____. If our understanding is incorrect, please let us know by _____ date."

If it is not on the inventory list for the boat, new or used, then it does not come with the boat. There is a reason on used boats that the listing with inventory is made part of the contract and signed by both parties. Things that are bolted to the boat, like heads, aren't usually listed, but anything that can get picked up and moved should be on the inventory list. In boat broker language, we talk about the items that will "convey with the vessel". Often a seller will have some items aboard that they don't want to take off until the boat is sold. These will not be listed and should be on a separate list of "items aboard that will NOT convey with vessel." When we sold our Skye, we kept two of the very expensive high tech winch handles (still left three handles aboard) and about $2,000 of other miscellaneous hardware that will be useful whenever we get our next boat, and we listed these items as "not conveying with vessel."

A reminder to ask about taxes and insurance: Once you have made an offer on the boat, it is a good idea to confirm your insurance and a boat slip. The insurance company may need to know where you intend to keep the boat in order to give you an estimate. When shopping for insurance, make sure you are comparing apples to apples on what your policy will cover; only get insurance for your immediate needs, not what you plan to do in the future. Ask your insurance agent to explain the difference between the amount you paid for the boat (Agreed value) and depreciated value after the purchase (Actual cash value), as well as deductibles and coverage for lightening strikes and named storms.

You will also need to be prepared to pay sales tax either to the state in which you live, or to the state in which you are buying the boat. This is often a separate transaction from the financing, so remember to ask your lender for the details. You may want to check with a lawyer, as well as an accountant, to find out the details on taxes.

Why you need to name your boat, even before you have completed the purchase.

All this time you have been dreaming of buying a boat. Have you also been thinking of what to name it? Keep in mind as you choose a name that your boat name will become your family name(s) to all the other cruisers. For example, we were Jeff & Jean Polyphonic.

There was one couple we worked with who have always gone with the name that the boat had when purchased and told us they have had some interesting questions about how they came up with the name of their boat. So far, no one has come up with a boat-naming book, like a list of baby names, so you will need to think of a name.

Try checking out a website http://10000boatnames.com. The site lists names alphabetically, so you can browse to your heart's delight. Remember you need to be hailed on the VHF radio. Try saying the name three times like someone was hailing you on the radio. It should be easy to spell and easy for the bridge tender to understand when you give him your name.

Example: We were sailing a boat named Makani U'I, after Beautiful Wind in Hawaiian, and when we hailed a bridge tender in Louisiana with the name, he repeated back "makin' who high?" We had to spell it out every time, multiple times.

Here's a list of some of the most common boat names in order of popularity:
  Second Wind   Serenity   Summer Wind   Serendipity
  Orion   Escape   Whisper   Carpe Diem   Calypso
  Camelot   Wind Song   Wind Dancer

By the way, while you're thinking of a name for the mother ship, check out names for the dinghy that matches the boat name like "China Doll and Tea Cup", "Polyphonic and Monotone", "Quietly and Noisy."

The name and hailing port is often fixed to the hull with stick on letters, which can be easily removed and replaced with the new name and hailing port.

Congratulations! You have a signed contract and you are now proud boat owners.

Here's the next 10 things you need to do:

1. Bill of Sale: You should have a "bill of sale" that you will need to register the boat. Be prepared to pay sales tax at this time when you go to the Division of Motor Vehicles (DMV.)

2. USCG Documentation: If you plan on cruising out of the U.S. at anytime in the future, you will need to have the boat U.S. Coast Guard Documented. Check with www.GloriaRector.com for title search and assistance with the documentation process.

3. Name of Boat. You will need to choose the name and give it to the documentation company at the time you submit the paperwork, so that you don't have to spend more money later going through the process of making a name change.

4. Lettering and name change: Get the lettering made and change the name on the boat. The USCG requires this, and has a stiff penalty if the name does not match the paperwork.

5. Reference the findings from your survey report and evaluate how to address them.

6. Make a list of all the things you think you want to do to the boat like: added equipment, new canvas, bottom paint, additional safety gear, life raft or offshore flares, dinghy and outboard. Get yourself a West Marine catalog and start to look up prices on each of the items and get estimates on the installation of this equipment.

7. Make a spreadsheet, so that you can then prioritize by importance the things you will actually install. We suggest listing items by must haves, like to have and, if we have enough left in our kitty, "nice to have."

8. Move the boat to her new home. If the vessel is more than a two-day journey to her new home, we recommend that you hire a professional delivery captain to relocate the boat. These captains have the experience of jumping on a boat completely unfamiliar to them and taking off to sea. This is not something we recommend to those that have never done it before!

9. Set up your maintenance log and schedule engine service; line up a diver to clean the bottom, regularly, too.

10. Shop for reliable vendors to begin working on your repair or upgrade list. Please ask for three quotes from different vendors so you can determine the best value, which may not necessarily be the least expensive.

Happy new boat owner's

They say the three happiest days in a boat owner's life are:
The day they buy the boat,
The day they sell the boat,
…. And the day their best friend buys a boat!

STEP 3 Checklist

1. You understand the design differences between Coastal and Bluewater and selected the category you need.

2. You have made a spreadsheet to keep track of which boats have what equipment to comparison shop.

3. You have compared at least three different brands of boat and have decided between Monohull (Center Cockpit/Aft Cockpit) and Catamaran.

4. You have made a budget for the boat (new or used, finance or cash). You have contacted a yacht finance professional to get loan information to give you more flexibility on your yacht choices.

5. You know what basic equipment, interior and exterior features you want. You have made a spreadsheet to compare yachts and equipment.

6. You have a budget for adding equipment and any needed repairs.

7. You have contacted a buyers broker to act on your behalf through the purchase process and selected a surveyor.

8. You have contacted an insurance agent.

9. You have decided on a name for the boat.

10. You have made plans for dockage and maintenance after the purchase.

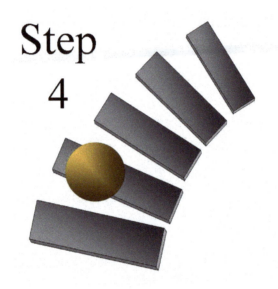

Step 4

Learn your boat

STEP 4 Learn your boat.

"Chick A Lou": Learning their Beneteau 43

How to get familiar with your boat.

OMG! You bought a boat. Let's pick up with the checklist we left you with at the end of Step 3 with our explanation of the purchase process. We will assume that you have sent in your paperwork for documentation, have insurance, and have moved the boat to her new home. In this section, we will review your systems training from your previous courses and give you a practice cruising guide for getting to know your new boat. We recommend you get familiar with your boat and her systems before you start on your list of any additional items you want to install. At the end of this chapter, we'll give you tips on budgeting and finding a vendor to install any additional equipment.

In order to start getting comfortable with your boat and all its systems, buy a label gun and a Sharpie and then go back to the Captain's checklist and go through your boat, locate the systems and begin making diagrams (unless you are lucky enough to have manuals from the manufacturer). Just take a regular spiral notebook and hand-draw an outline of the boat hull.

Start by lifting up every floorboard and going underneath every berth. Empty out all of the lockers, and clean them while you are at it. As you locate the tankage, batteries, motors and pumps, you will want to make a note of the details, so as you find spare parts, you may also be able to identify what they go to and log this information carefully. See example systems diagram below.

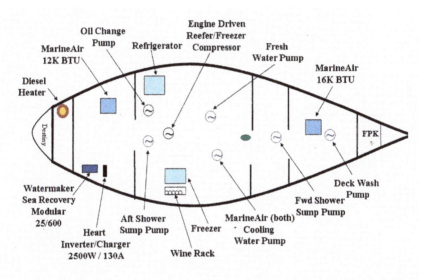

SYSTEMS

This may seem overwhelming at first, but by taking the time to draw out the location of each of these items, you will know exactly where each tank, pump, motor and battery is located and what type, size and capacity they hold.

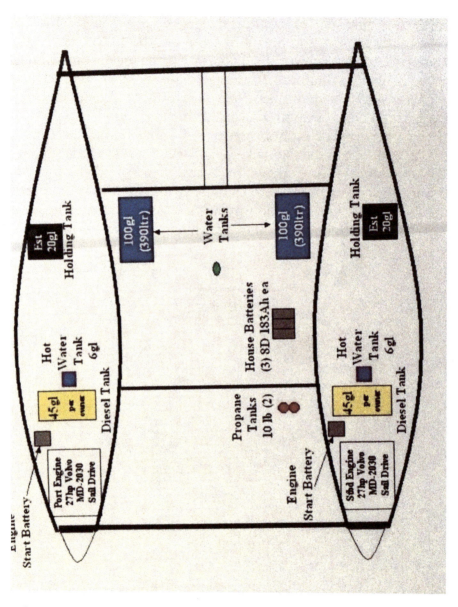

Above is an example of a diagram of tankage for a catamaran. It is just a matter of investigating underneath every berth and floorboard and reading the labels on each of the tanks to get the manufacturers specifications of capacity.

Continue with these important diagrams

After you locate the fuel and water tanks, locate the deck fills that match each tank and label them. Code the fresh water deck fill with blue tape, waste pump out with black and the diesel fill cap with yellow. This will keep you from maybe putting water in the diesel or diesel in the water.

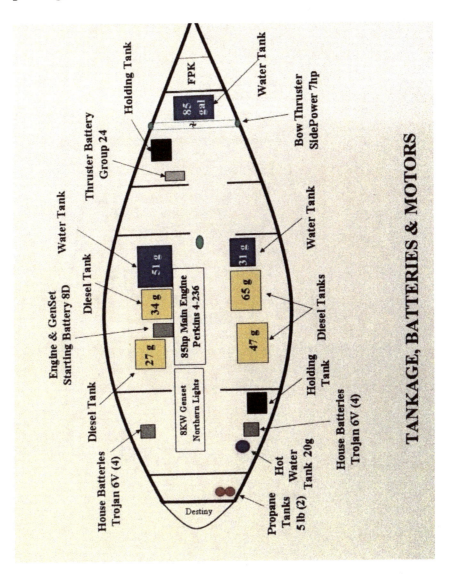

You will need to track down every thru hull in the boat so you can understand the status and function of each of the valves, open or closed. In addition, you need to locate all of the sea strainers, so that they can be serviced. Below is an example of catamaran thru hull diagram.

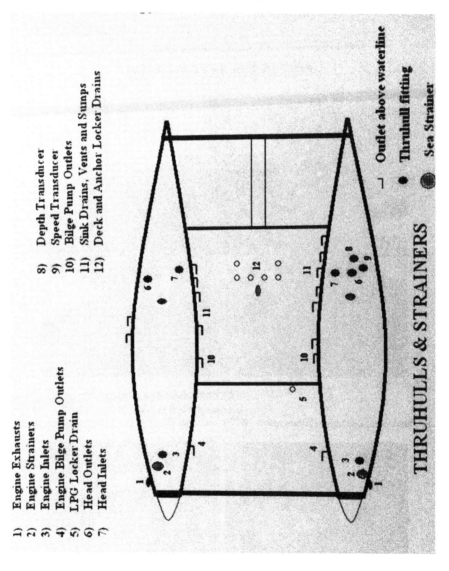

Pictured here is the monohull thru hull diagram example. Did you realize just how many thru hulls are in a modern cruising boat?

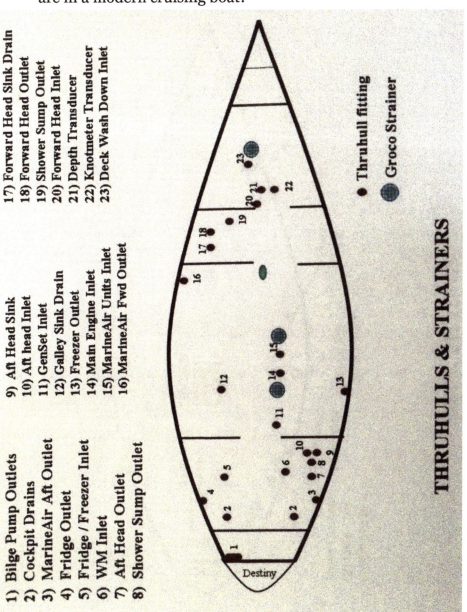

17) Forward Head Sink Drain
18) Forward Head Outlet
19) Shower Sump Outlet
20) Forward Head Inlet
21) Depth Transducer
22) Knotmeter Transducer
23) Deck Wash Down Inlet

9) Aft Head Sink
10) Aft head Inlet
11) GenSet Inlet
12) Galley Sink Drain
13) Freezer Outlet
14) Main Engine Inlet
15) MarineAir Units Inlet
16) MarineAir Fwd Outlet

1) Bilge Pump Outlets
2) Cockpit Drains
3) MarineAir Aft Outlet
4) Fridge Outlet
5) Fridge / Freezer Inlet
6) WM Inlet
7) Aft Head Outlet
8) Shower Sump Outlet

• Thruhull fitting
● Groco Strainer

THRUHULLS & STRAINERS

After a thorough sorting, make a designated place for tools and important supplies for repair and maintenance. When you need a hose clamp, you don't want to try and remember into which toolbox you stuck the spares. Discipline yourself to keep things like hose clamps and caulk in one place, and to put them back in the same place every time.

Now that you have cleaned out the boat and made a place for tools and supplies for maintenance and repairs, you should have room to stow your galley supplies and provisions. As you start to use the boat over the first month, you will find that you may have to relocate some of the things you stored.

Once you are settled in, go back to the notebook and log your personal inventory. This will save you time and money in the long run. For example, in the diagrams on the previous pages you can see where the water pressure pump is located. You found a spare pump and have room to stow it in the forward stateroom portside locker, so make a note in your logbook that this is where you placed it. If this pump fails, a replacement runs about $275 to $300 just for the pump. The diagram could tell us that the hose connectors are stored there as well. If you stowed it and did not log it, you will go on a hunting expedition, give up, then go buy another pump.

Understanding your boat's systems and equipment.

Now that you have started lifting all of the floorboards and made diagrams of where pumps and batteries are located you may realize that you need more than just sailing knowledge. You also need a thorough understanding of the systems on the boat. You should have received some systems experience during your bareboat charter course. Read through these basic systems descriptions and find out if you have any holes in your education. Then you will know what you should learn to be safe while out cruising.

There was a time when cruising boats were very simple, and there are some that still espouse that style of cruising. This is not right or wrong, just a different approach to the lifestyle. Sailors and authors Lin and Larry Pardey are the best examples of the simplest cruising style and for those of you seeking this minimalist style, their books should be referenced. Steve and Linda Dashew, authors of *The Offshore Cruising Encyclopedia,* represent the other end of this spectrum. They circumnavigated in a 65 foot yacht, and then moved up to an 82 foot yacht with every system one could imagine.

Most of the cruisers we see out there are somewhere in between these two examples. The majority of the couples we meet who retire to cruise want a boat with systems that allow a life style more similar to their life ashore than to camping out, but this comes at a cost.

With the proliferation of systems to give us the comforts we wish for, comes the maintenance and overhead of keeping up with them. In the early years of sailing, we'd sign off letters to cruisers with, "May you have Fair Winds and Smooth Seas" Now we sign off with, "May you have Fair Winds and Smooth Working Systems."

When a system does fail, you must decide if you can, or wish to fix it yourself or call that magic phone number 1-800-FIX-THAT. Of course, if you are in the Out Islands of the Bahamas, the phone number won't work very well.

Boat systems can have strong personalities and like a pet cat, they won't change to match yours, you must adapt to them. If you take the time to get basic training on the different systems and to get to know your boat you will find a harmony that keeps everything working smoothly.

In this section, we will highlight those systems we feel are critical, the ones for which you should have basic training and an understanding of their care and feeding.

Diesel Engine Operations and Maintenance

When you take responsibility for a charter boat, the charter company expects that you will monitor the engine for proper operation to prevent any damage. Now that you have bought your own boat, understanding engine operation means even more, as little problems can become big expensive problems. You should know how to check the fluids, the oil and closed cooling water systems to make sure the engine has the proper fluid levels. Adding too much oil can be as problematic as too little oil. So have an understanding of what the right level is and know when you should check the engine fluids. You do not have to be a diesel mechanic, but you should know that the diesel engine needs four things to run: a battery for power to start, clean fuel, oil and cooling water. After you have purchased the boat, it is a good idea to hire a diesel mechanic to do an oil change and go over the engine with you so you can get the basics on your boat engine and have a starting point for your maintenance log.

Checking the water flow out of the stern of the boat is a simple way of knowing if the raw water-cooling system is working. You should check the water flow every time you start the engine and periodically when you are motoring. Water should be flowing.

Things that can happen: Example #1
We were sailing with Jill and Jack on their Vagabond 47, going from Stuart FL to Buffalo NY. While in the Erie Canal, the water stopped flowing from the engine and the temperature gauge began to climb. We quickly turned off the engine, dropped the anchor, and went into diagnostic mode. The issue turned out to be a clogged thru-hull. We used an air pump to blast it clear and in less than an hour were on our way again with no problems. The new owners were feeling major anxiety when the engine "failed", but we were able to keep them calm and teach them how to quickly diagnose and solve the problem.

Vagabond 47 "Black Swan" transiting the Erie Canal

Example # 2:
We once chartered a catamaran in Belize and noticed that the water flow on the port engine was not as strong as the flow on the starboard engine. The charter company employee giving our boat briefing mentioned that flow appeared to be "normal" for this boat. As we motored along the following day, we noticed less water and some white smoke on the port engine exhaust. We decided to pull over and drop the anchor to check the sea strainer and see if we had picked up some seaweed, or determine if something else was clogging the strainer. After we were anchored we opened the sea strainer and discovered that the hoses to the strainer basket were reversed.

We called the charter company and asked if some one had recently installed new hoses. Indeed, they had installed new hoses; however, they installed them backwards. We suggested, with their permission, that we switch the hoses. We did and guess what, good water flow! The engine raw water sea strainer was now correctly connected and everything was back to proper working order. This simple problem was solved, but if not corrected, it could have had disastrous results.

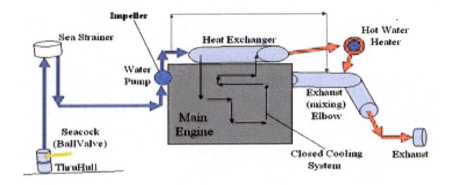

Engine Cooling Polyphonic

Above is a diagram of our engine cooling system.

Where and when you can go to learn more about diesel engines.

Up north, when it is too cold for sailing, or down south, when it is too hot for sailing, is a good time to invest in a course on diesel engines. There are two good sources we recommend where you can go to get hands on training on the basics: The Annapolis School of Seamanship and Mack Boring both offer detailed courses of anywhere from one to three days. These schools provide training on components and operation, the lubrication system, the fuel system, the cooling system and performing basic maintenance. We highly recommend that both you and your sailing partner take a course on marine diesel engines.

Tankage: Potable Water, Fuel and Waste Systems

The potable water or drinking water on board most cruising boats today operates through a battery (DC) powered fresh water pressure pump. When you flip the breaker switch to turn on the fresh water pump, you should hear the pump cycle on. Hearing the pump will make you aware that the system is active. When you leave the boat, be in the habit of turning off the breaker for the water pressure to keep the pump from running, should there be a leak in the system. For example, let's say the boat is equipped with two or three water tanks. When one tank runs out, the pump will continue to run until you switch to another tank. If you aren't monitoring the system you could burn out the pump. If the pump keeps cycling on and off, most likely there is a small drip somewhere; perhaps someone has just left a head sink knob loose. It really is a lot of common sense, but you need to understand these things if you want to have a pleasant, uneventful trip.

If you are in a cruising area where you have limited resources, you should practice conservation techniques. This could mean washing the dishes with seawater and then rinsing with a small amount of fresh water, or showering only after a swim, using the shower on the transom. At the very least, make sure everyone on board is aware of his or her water usage. If you have clear tanks, you should visually inspect the tank levels daily. It is also a good idea to bring some bottled water for emergency use. What if the pump fails? Can you get the water out of the tank another way, perhaps with a manual pump? We once had our DC powered fresh water pressure pump fail. We had 200 gallons of water in the tanks, but could not access it, so we had no water until we reached port. After that experience, we never leave without backup water in bottles.

Tracking the fuel level.

Many boats these days are equipped with a fuel gauge, which may or may not work. Prior to your departure on any long journey, you should have some kind of idea what the engine fuel consumption rate is, and be able to estimate how much fuel you think you will need for your trip. Once you are under way, keep track of how many hours you use the engine. Log the engine hours at the start of the trip and then again each and every morning. If there is a gauge, note what it reads, get to know how your fuel gauge operates. Start out by filling your fuel tank to the top, make sure it is really full. Watch the fuel gauge carefully and check to see what it reads. Make a log entry to keep track of how much fuel was pumped and what the gauge read before and after pumping. Over time and through logging engine hours between tank fills you will get to know your boat and how much fuel it uses.

We have tried to explain to many new boat shoppers that the size of the fuel tank is an important factor to consider when buying the boat. If you plan on day sailing and short trips along the coast, a small tank will suffice. However, if you plan on cruising to the Caribbean and perhaps beyond, you will motor more than you expect. In order to cruise comfortably, you want to give yourselves plenty of options along the way. You need to know your range under power.

Example: One time while cruising from Puerto Rico to the West Coast of Florida, the trade winds failed and all we could do was drift and wait, because our range under power was about 500 miles and we had a thousand miles to go. Fuel was our limiting factor. Since there was no place to refuel, we had to conserve. If we'd a larger fuel tank, we could have motored until the wind came in.

Here's an example of a power distribution panel.

The power budget basics and understanding AC & DC power

The batteries are the direct current DC or 12-volt systems that power the things you need to operate the boat while underway: the navigation equipment, VHF radio, cabin lights, night navigation lights, water pump and more. Most of the new cruising boats also run the refrigeration from the batteries.

The batteries are wired to the DC breaker panel that distributes power to the various systems. To turn off the water pressure pump, for example, just turn off the breaker at the panel. The boat may also be equipped with a 12 volt or cigarette lighter style outlet, also powered by the boat's batteries, that you can use to charge small devices like your cell phone. You may also find a 12-volt outlet right on the main panel.

You should know how the batteries are wired. Most boats will have at least two batteries or banks of batteries; one to run the systems on the boat (known as the House Bank) and one dedicated to starting the engine. Understand that both battery banks can usually be linked together by a battery switch enabling you to combine the batteries. You should find the switch and note whether it is set for one, two or both sets of batteries.

The alternating current (AC) system operates high power draw systems, such as the battery charger, the hot water tank (when it is heated electrically), the air conditioners, and the outlets that feed devices like a microwave oven or plug-in coffee pot. These items will operate just as they do in your land home when plugged into shore power or with a generator when sufficient power is applied. The shore power is plugged into the boat from the outside and provides power to the AC breaker panel. There should be a light or a gauge at the breaker panel that tells you the boat is receiving power. If the boat is equipped with a generator, there should be an additional switch that will prevent you from getting AC power from both shore power and the generator at the same time; it's one or the other.

Example:
Ian and Irene were at anchor on their way down the Chesapeake Bay on their second week of cruising. They were learning about electricity, the batteries, and generator. Ian had the generator running, all of the reverse cycle heat/air conditioners running on full heat, and the battery charger on bulk charge. All together these systems were using at least 4,500 watts. Ian forgot they weren't hooked to the shore power grid, but were generating their own power with a 5,000-watt generator. When he placed the coffee mug in the 1000-watt microwave and hit "Start" there was a gzzzzt sound and everything went dark. After going through a checklist we provided for them, our phone rang and it was Ian, a bit sheepish since he knew he was making a mistake the moment after he hit "Start." We walked him through a diagnostic path and eventually determined that a fuse built into the generator itself had blown. Once the fuse was changed with a spare, everything powered back up just fine.

Keeping track of your power usage and battery state should become part of your everyday living.

You should have a basic understanding of battery capacity and charging systems through either the boat's alternator on the main engine or through shore power to a charger. Think of the batteries in terms of tankage, just like a water tank. The size of the tank equals the capacity and how long it takes to refill that tank is the charging factor. What you need to know is what capacity the batteries have and how long it takes for the charging source to replenish the batteries.

Because you need to know the status of the batteries, the boat will need to have a battery monitoring system. Most boats are equipped with a gauge on the DC breaker panel that shows battery voltage. The gauge only gives you a coarse status of the batteries, 11.5-volts (almost dead) to 14-volts (maximum charge). It does not reveal how much power is being drawn. It is a good habit to check the battery status when you are just under sail, so that you do not wait too long to fire up the engine to recharge. Now that you own your boat, you will want a monitoring system, like those offered by Magnum or Xantrex, which can tell you how much current each device draws. With these monitors, you will have the insight into your electrical systems you need for easy and comfortable voyaging.

What you should know about other power sources.
Another source of AC (120v) power besides shore power and generator is the inverter.

The use of an inverter is the most misunderstood of these electrical systems by those new to the boating life. To simplify: an inverter draws power from the battery and can enable an AC (120v) device plugged into an outlet to operate. However, if the device draws more power than the battery can provide, you can drain the battery down to nothing in an instant. A few uses of a hair dryer and those battery banks will be flat dead. This is why most charter boats do not have an inverter and if they do, it will be very small, just enough for charging cell phones or computers. Improper use of the inverter is the fastest way to kill your batteries.

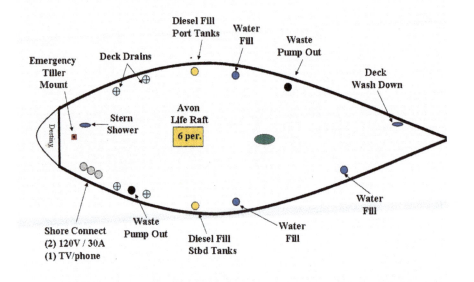

DECK FITTINGS

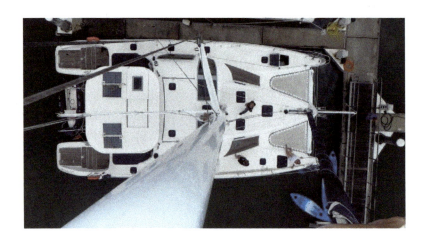

Sailboat standing and running rigging, furling gear & winches

It is essential to monitor both the standing and running rigging. Learn how to look carefully for any tarnishing of the stainless steel chain plates, turnbuckles or wire. This could be a sign of a weakening in the standing rigging. On the running rigging watch for chafe or fraying of the lines as they turn through the blocks, look for weak spots and for any place where the jib sheets may get caught or rub when you tack.

Think of what you would do if a halyard broke or a jib sheet snapped. Make a plan and then discuss it. Check to see what spare lines are available should something happen. Look at how the hardware is run on the boat. You should be able to move the cars on the track to adjust the angle of the jib sheets when you furl a reef into the genoa. You should understand how an override on a winch can occur and how to clear it. Check out how and where the winches are located. Think through a tack and a jibe and how to handle each line. Understand how the furling gear works for the jib and the main, if you have a furling mainsail. Hopefully you have labeled all the clutches by now, so you know which line goes to what.

Example: *A catamaran that we sailed on had one winch on the starboard side and one winch on the port side. The mainsheet was run through a clutch, and the boat did not have a way of putting the sheet on a winch when jibing. We like to have more control of the main during a jibe especially if it is a large sail by having the main sheet on a winch. In our opinion, many of the new production boats do not have enough winches and if this were our boat, we would add another winch. Often, on the monohull boats we sail, the jib furling line has no dedicated winch. You can use a winch if on the opposite tack of where the furling line is led. Be observant of how the running rigging is set up and think ahead how to use the winches most effectively. Consider whether you want to add a winch or other deck hardware.*

What you need to know about your Chartplotter, GPS, VHF and Autopilot

You should take some time to understand how your navigation system is wired. For example, you need to turn on the power source for the GPS first, because it feeds data to both the chartplotter and the VHF radio and the boat needs to know where it is before you can use these tools.

Understand the "Vessel Position" on your chartplotter, versus the "Cursor Position." It's critical to your safety that both sailing partners know exactly how to find both cursor and vessel position on the system you have installed. If one of you is incapacitated, the other will need this knowledge. We frequently see what happens when both partners in a cruising couple are not proficient.

Example*:*
One of the boats was having trouble in strong winds bouncing around some mud banks. Each time the captain hailed her position to us, it was 5 nautical miles in a different direction from the previous hail. We knew she was reading position from her plotter, so for a moment, we wondered how she was moving so fast and then it dawned on us, she was reading Cursor Position.

Now, you old salts and technophiles out there are snorting at this as being silly, but the average experience level out there today is very low. New cruisers are overwhelmed with all the things they are learning to handle on the 40+foot boat they just bought and they need things to be as simple as possible, especially those skills needed in an emergency when brain freeze may effect reactions.

What to do? The first thing we do to any chartplotter when we get on a boat is configure the data boxes so Vessel Position is always displayed and is obvious, preferably in the upper left corner, since Westerners are taught to read starting there. We wish the electronics manufacturers would ship them with this configuration as the default.

Plan on spending time at the dock, pushing the buttons on your chartplotter, to learn how to operate it. Today's modern navigation tools are complex and dangerous if you do not realize that the accuracy of the data is dependent on the zoom level. For example, on one chartplotter, we used a large mud bank, known as Featherbed in Biscayne Bay, which completely disappears from the chart at a two mile zoom level and only shows up on the screen at one mile. So give yourself enough time to review actual paper charts and compare them to your plotter to see when the details disappear.

Very High Frequency (VHF)

Here is another equally vital tip: never leave the dock before checking that the VHF radio is working. Look at the radio base station and see if it has the correct GPS position displayed. If it does not show position, the emergency Red Distress button is useless. The new VHF radios have a Digital Distress Signal built in; however, if the radio is not connected to the ship's GPS, it does not know your location.

Secondly, if the owner has not registered the radio, the ship's information cannot be transmitted. If you notice that the GPS is not connected, you should also assume it has no automated system. We put tape over the Distress button to remind us that it will not work. This means you will need to know your GPS position to call for help. Practice figuring out the vessel's position and be sure each member of the crew understands how to find it. By now, you should have used the VHF to call marinas, bridges and other vessels. This is an essential safety skill.

We believe that it is critical for couples to have a VHF remote microphone (mic) mounted near the helm, so that if one person is incapacitated, the other can stay at the helm and call for help. In addition to calling for help, you should understand how important it is that you monitor the VHF. If you have to hail a Mayday, you certainly hope someone will be listening.

If you can't spend the few extra dollars to put a proper remote mic from your base station VHF in your cockpit so that you can hear and respond to your "neighbor's" mayday, why should you expect that they would hear yours? Note: A handheld VHF is not a substitute for having a remote mic from your ship's VHF. VHF is line of sight and your ship's unit has the antenna at the masthead 50-feet or 60-feet+ high and broadcasts at 25 watts, yielding a range of 30 nautical miles or more. Handheld VHF broadcasts at 5 watts and is only 6-feet above the water and usually only reaches one to two nautical miles.

Example #1: Rasta Captain Ron Lost?

On a run across the Anegada Passage from St. Martin to Virgin Gorda rolling a hundred miles downwind, we got to meet what we now jokingly call the "Rasta Captain Ron." About half way across we heard a Mayday call on our cockpit speaker. Coast Guard (USCG) Puerto Rico responded "Vessel in Distress, what is the nature of your emergency?" The vessel responded, "My crew is sick and I need a tow to St. Martin." This was interesting since there is no one that will tow you half way across the Anegada passage. The USCG handed the call off to Virgin Islands Search and Rescue (VISAR), and they learned from the vessel that the crew was just seasick and they were lost on their way to St. Martin because their GPS had failed. VISAR got their last known position. As we listened in, we realized they were downwind of us and not far off our course. We contacted VISAR and offered to work the vessel for them, which they gladly accepted. We then asked the vessel what course and speed they'd been making since their last known GPS position and plotted a circle of "probable position," then headed for the windward side of this circle. When we arrived, we found a 35-foot charter sloop being skippered by a local captain delivering it to St. Martin from Virgin Gorda. He was doing donuts waiting for us to arrive. It was too rough for us to pull along side, so we got close enough to toss a baggie containing our position on a piece of paper, some Dramamine, and a fishing sinker to give the baggie some throwing weight. The baggie hit the boat right near the Rasta captain's hand, but in the roll of the boat, he missed grabbing the baggie and it bounced overboard, whereupon, he sagged in frustration. Meanwhile, Jean stood on our deck and noted that she could see the island of Saba to windward. Saba is just southwest of St. Martin, and when you are near it, you can see St. Martin and can then adjust course. Jean hailed our Rasta Captain calling, "Hey, man! You can see Saba!" He jumped on his deck, standing tall, and pointed at the conical volcanic island in the distance, "That's Saba?" Jean said, "Yes, that's Saba!" In a flash, with a quick thank you, our Rasta Captain Ron throttled up to full speed and was last seen motoring over the horizon towards Saba. We hailed VISAR to tell them the problem had been taken care of and they thanked us.

Example #2: A lost diver.

During an ASA 104 class on an Out Island 41 on Biscayne Bay we were sailing on a fine day when we heard a Mayday call on the VHF. The vessel's captain reported, with amazing calmness, that his son had been diving and could not be found. He had been missing long enough that Dad was now calling for help. With professionalism, he reported the circumstances and the vessel's position. We noted that we were near by and just to leeward of him. We hailed him and confirmed that he was the dark hulled yacht we could see about a mile to windward.

We struck sail, letting the father and the Coast Guard know that we were assisting and went into search mode -- zigzagging our way upwind. We were in a good position to help, since it was most likely that his son had drifted down wind from their boat. After about 20 minutes, the captain hailed saying that his son had been found. It seems the son had spotted a friend's boat, swam over and took off without letting Dad know. We were all happy it ended well, and wondered just what words those two would have that evening!

You never know when you may be the one in a position to help. Have the VHF set up so you can use it in the cockpit. Also, if you need help, you may not be able to go below; being able to call from the cockpit could mean the difference between being saved... or not.

Autopilot

The autopilot is an absolute "must have" piece of equipment for couples out cruising today. Practice using the autopilot in various wind and sea conditions; take note if the autopilot has any difficulty.

The best autopilot systems will steer through some very rough conditions that you may not be able to handle physically. We have found that an autopilot connected directly to the rudderpost works best, and it is your first means of emergency steering, if the steering cables break. Check your instruments to monitor your course over ground; make sure the autopilot compass matches your ship's compass.

Once, we were the first people to charter a boat that had been delivered under sail all the way from South Africa, with the autopilot flux gate compass (which is the one tied to the autopilot) misaligned 25 degrees from the ship's compass. So the chartplotter displayed the vessel going sideways. Watch for our next book, "OMG! We bought a boat," where we will tell you how to tune your instruments. It is unfortunate that so many boats do not receive proper commissioning; you will be expected to know what your position is, even if the three compasses on board do not agree.

There are many cool things a modern autopilot can do that really help couples cruising. For instance, the autopilot could be used to change course through a tack or hold the boat into the wind leaving you both free to handle the lines.

Safety equipment: a basic guide

We strongly recommend that you attend a Safety At Sea seminar, where you can learn the difference between coastal and offshore flares, as well as how to use both flares and a fire extinguisher.

When you board a boat that is new to you, check the location and status of the emergency equipment. Find the flares and check the dates to be sure they have not expired. Find out where, and how many, fire extinguishers are on board. Check to see if the gauges read in the green. Check the fire extinguishers to see if the chemical is stuck on the bottom. If so, it most likely doesn't work. You may even consider buying new fire extinguishers, so that you know you are starting with known good equipment. Write the date of purchase on the fire extinguishers and fill out the inspection tag that comes with it in the box to start your own annual inspection.

Locate the first aid kit and check to see whether it contains essentials such as: Band-Aids and aspirin or what ever pain or fever relief medication you use; antibacterial cream; scissors; sea-sickness pills, etc. We recommend that you take a Red Cross first aid course to give you a refresher on the most current methods. In addition, they will help you learn how to stock your first aid kit.

We also recommend the vessel be equipped with an "abandon ship" bag (ACR makes an excellent "Rapid Ditch" bag). It should contain the following: Emergency Position Indicator Radio Beacon or EPIRB. (you will need to register this in your name and with your contact info); a 25mm flare gun with a minimum of 3 meteor & 2 parachute flares (25mm or safety of life at sea SOLAS certified for offshore work); 3 hand flares; signal mirror; whistle, thermal blanket; glow sticks, sealable plastic bags for crew ID/Passports/wallets; water dye; hand fishing line & lure; spare GPS; spare VHF; satellite phone and other signaling devices.

The Life Raft: regardless of whether your boat came with a life raft or was not already equipped with one, you will want a life raft. There are many different life rafts on the market, and we recommend that you wait and take your time to select the right one for you and your cruising plans. If you will be near shore, a coastal life raft may be suitable; however, if you are planning to sail across oceans, you will need an offshore raft that provides shelter and is capable of sustaining you for weeks instead of hours. We want you to also get familiar with your boat and systems before you head offshore. Your life raft requires regular servicing and repacking, which can run anywhere from $800 to $1200 or more. By waiting until you are really ready to depart for distant shores you can ensure the most up to date service.

Once again, we highly recommend that you both participate in at least one Safety At Sea seminar. There is no substitute for seeing a flare set off or a life raft deployed. It is even more memorable when you can get into a life raft in the water and try it out.

By now, you should have invested in your own safety harnesses and life jackets, as well as a hand held GPS and VHF. Good foul weather gear should be something you invest in, as well. There is no substitute for having proper personal gear.

When we assist couples in getting familiar with their new boat, we bring along what we call the captain's bag, equipped with GPS, VHF, Navigation tools, binoculars, SPOT (a personal EPRIB) and a sealed plastic bag with a few spare hose clamps, Atomic or Rescue tape, wooden bungs to plug a leaking thru hull fitting, and small pieces of line. Although we can't fly with flares, we can assume the yacht will have them, but these basic items allow us to be prepared, in case the yacht is not fully equipped, or if it suffers from equipment failure. As a boat owner, you need to learn to be prepared and make your own safety gear checklist.

What you should know about the outboard and dinghy.

You should both know how to start the outboard and operate the dinghy. These allow you the freedom to go ashore. Be aware that the outboard will have the most "personality" of any of the systems on your boat, so give yourself time to learn the tempo of your outboard. You should have the basic knowledge that a 2-stroke engine requires oil mixed in with the gas, and a 4 stroke outboard engine has an oil reservoir. You should know that water in the gas may foul the tank and prevent the outboard from running. Know the basic use of the choke and the engine kill switch. You should also both be trained in your emergency plan if the outboard engine dies while you are not attached to the mother ship. Remember, the dinghy is another boat, and it needs to be equipped with its own safety equipment.

Dinghy in the dark

Example: When we first bought our cruising boat, we had never really had a dinghy, so it was nice to be able to anchor out and take the dinghy into town. On our very first night at anchor, we treated ourselves to a night on the town, got dressed up and took the dinghy into the town dock. We locked her to the dock and had a lovely night on the town. When we returned to the dock it was dark; we unlocked the dinghy, fired up the outboard and headed out in search of our boat at anchor. All of a sudden, the engine died and we were adrift; the paddles were stowed in a cooler and turned out to only be half a paddle. The tiny anchor was all snarled up in the line, which was not long enough for the depth of the water. So Jeff wound up swimming the dinghy back to our boat. After that very scary incident, we learned our lesson: the dinghy is a boat. Never head off without paddles, an anchor, small flare packet, life jackets, hand held VHF at a minimum; we even pack a bag with water and snacks and more if we are in a more remote area.

Systems Summary

We want you to be well-educated users of the systems on your boat. By now, you have hopefully labeled the deck hardware, created some diagrams, located your batteries, tankage, pump, etc., as well as other items needing maintenance and created your own log for tracking. When you encounter equipment failure, you'll know if it is operator error or if it is actually the product failing.

Take the time to learn these systems for safe, enjoyable voyages

A good source of general knowledge on boat systems is Liza Copeland's book *Cruising For Cowards from A to Z.*

Systems knowledge checklist

1. You have an understanding of how Diesel engines work and know the fuel system.

2. You understand the Potable water system from tank to pressure pump, including how the hot water tank is heated.

3. You understand how the head plumbing operates, manual or electric pump to the holding tank, emptied by thru hull, macerator or deck pump out.

4. You understand the refrigeration system, how it is powered either by cold plate (AC powered) with water cooled pump or battery (DC powered) with air-cooled pump.

5. You know the basic electrical systems, AC Shore power, Generator (Genset), Inverter, as well as DC power, Batteries, Amp hours, capacity, charging and monitoring.

6. You understand the basics of sailboat rigging, standing and running, and have overall knowledge of furling gear and winches and their safe operation.

7. You can operate the Chartplotter, GPS, VHF and autopilot.

8. You have attended a "Safety At Sea" seminar and know how to deploy a flare and use a fire extinguisher.

9. You have your own Life jacket with harness and tether.

10. You have a basic understanding of the safe operation of an outboard motor.

Recommended Equipment Checklist

Abandon ship bag (ACR makes excellent "Rapid Ditch" Bag) containing:
 EPIRB, Flare Gun 25mm, 3 meteor & 2 parachute flares 25mm or SOLAS (3) Hand Flares, Signal Mirror, Whistle, Thermo Blanket, Glow sticks, Baggies for crew ID/Passports/ wallets Water dye, Hand fishing line & lure, spare GPS, spare handheld VHF, Other signaling devices, deck of cards.
Air Horn (portable can style) or installed with loud hailer
Rescue tape (which bonds to itself to repair high temp and high pressure hoses)
Fuel Funnel Filter (large) diesel (for filtering fuel as it goes in tank)
Barometer
Batteries (D, AA and any others needed for on board equipment)
Binoculars
Boat hook(s)
Bucket, brushes, rags, Soft Scrub
Bungee cords (at least one dozen mixed sizes)
Chafe gear, Velcro style (4+ pieces)
Digital Volt Meter
Dinghy, plus repair kit, foot pump, 2 tow lines and bridle, lifting tackle
Dock line (sized for boat: two bow, two stern, two springs+ spares)
Duct tape
Engine & Genset Spares:
    (Impellers, Belts, Oil, Coolant, Transmission fluid, Filters)
Ensign flag (w/staff?) (Etiquette is 1" flag length for each foot of vessel.)
FCC license (Radar, EPIRB, VHF, SSB) (needed for International travel only)
Fenders (4) Large size
First Aid Kit
     (Customized items for offshore see www.oceanmedix.com)
Flash Lights
Foul weather gear
Fuel filters

Recommended Equipment Checklist (cont.)

Hose clamps (mixed sizes)
Hydraulic Fluid
Inland Navigation Rules (USCG requires if over 40')
Jack lines (2 each 50'+)
Life Raft (6 person min.)
   (Winslow Life Rafts' guarantee to replace yours if you ever have to use it)
MMSI # for DSC VHF (apply via Boat U.S. or for Intl travel with FCC)
MOB Light (ACR or Forespar brands recommended)
Navigation tools:
 (Dividers, parallels, calculator, watch, pencils, light list, Chart1)
Notices: oil, garbage, propane
Oil absorbing pads (10)
Outboard motor for dinghy, plus:
(Oil, shear pins, grease, spark plugs, "mouse ears" for engine flush)
PB Blaster (freeing lubricant)
Radar reflector
 (Davis folding type works well, may consider permanent one instead)
Reflective Tape (for putting on life jackets and MOB gear)
Rigging Knife
Second Anchor & rode (sized for vessel)
SPOT personal EPIRB
(Can be used for sending text to family inexpensively while underway)
Spotlight (cordless)
Siphon hose (short hose w/check valve for transferring fuel)
Teflon plumbing tape
Tie wraps (UV protected type, small/medium sizes)
Tools (usual set + make sure proper diesel bleed wrenches)
Water hose (50' - 75' garden) with nozzle
WD40
Whistles (one for each life jacket)
Whipping twine (wax coated for finishing line ends)

How to test your systems to see if you are ready to go.

Okay, just remember, "Something is broken on your boat"; you just don't know it yet. You get over it! You will learn how to fix or repair almost everything yourselves over time.

Have patience and give yourselves the time to learn. Commit to an open mind to give yourselves enough time to ease into this new lifestyle. After a while you let go of your previous life style and relax naturally.

If you have taken your time to get to know your boat and her personality, she in turn will protect you and carry you both through many years of safe, comfortable cruising.

Now that you have a basic understanding of your boat systems, you may think you want to add more stuff. Before you spend the entire cruising kitty on all the cool stuff at the boat show, let us consider if you have actually left the dock and if you have tested these systems at anchor. How long have you gone disconnected from shore power?

One of the many cruising couples we worked with thought they were all ready to head off to the Bahamas. They invited us to use their boat as the lead boat in a flotilla and to have a final shake down. They had been living on board for six months at the dock while they continued to outfit the boat. On this shake down cruise, they discovered that the batteries were not able to keep a charge and their refrigeration was not adequate, so they were able to return to the dock, after the flotilla and address the issues.

After you learn the basic operation of your boat's systems, you need to test just how well everything performs when you stay at anchor. We will give you a few ideas on what you might want to test, and then you might want to reconsider your list of additions in a different order. Realize that your new lifestyle is on your timetable and no one else's timetable. Once you move aboard and untie your dock lines, you are cruising.

Our first cruise was just down the canal from our slip to the yacht club. The next hop was only about a six-hour sail to an anchorage and after a week, we began to relax. We were listening to the radio one afternoon. The announcer reporting the traffic said, "There was a big tie up on the freeway, what a mess", and we realized we had no worries. After three weeks we didn't even know what day of the week it was. Relax, and soon you will be thinking about where you want to sail next, based on which way the wind is blowing.

The next checklist is designed to help you determine how well you understand your power budget; that is to say, balancing system needs, electronics usage and your charging sources for your batteries. Test out your refrigeration while disconnected from shore power; place a thermometer inside and locate which are the cold spots and which part of the refrigerator is best for produce. You will also need to practice using your anchor tackle and windlass. Create your own hand signals for communication between bow and helm for both anchoring and docking. During these short test voyages, you should not plan to venture very far from your homeport. Try to choose a route that will allow you to day sail, and then anchor for the night. While you are sailing and using your electronic navigation tools, with the engine off, check the battery voltage. Later, after you are anchored, check to see how well the refrigeration is cooling and then check your battery voltage. Check the voltage again in the morning after you have been anchored and perhaps watched TV, played the stereo, and run the anchor light, as well as cabin lights.

Practice your anchoring techniques. Make notes on the speed at which the windlass paid out the chain. While you were watching the chain, did you see any markings on the length of chain? If the chain was unmarked, you will want to take time to mark it. We suggest a really simple code for the chain, since you most likely will never need less than 50' of chain. Make a green mark at 50', then a yellow mark at 75' and a red mark at 100', double red mark at 125'. As to how to mark the chain, we have tried it all, from paint to custom plastic pieces that fit in the links; what worked for us was colored plastic zip ties. They cost only a few dollars per multi-colored package. Sure, they break off over time, but they are simple to replace, easier than paint and less expensive than other products. The code is easy to remember green traffic light, go. Yellow light slow down and, you guessed it, red means stop.

Another note to make while practicing your anchoring is which way she backs down, and how much you need to adjust your set up position when you drop the anchor to accommodate for the prop walk. Check to see if you have enough chain and if you have a snubber line. If not, you may want to add these to your shopping list.

When you are sailing near home, you can also practice going out in bad weather. We found that practicing near home allows you the feeling of security, in that help is nearby. This reduces the fear factor, when your home slip is close at hand, and reduces the stress that handling bad weather usually causes. You can start out with some heavier winds and progress your skills over time, even if you only practice for a few hours at a time. See how both you and your partner can adjust sails according to conditions. Test out the reefing system; see how difficult it is to furl the genoa in a blow. This will help you determine if you need to add a clutch or change a sheeting angle, buy some additional deck hardware, etc. Plus by testing the sailing systems under load, you will know how the boat and equipment respond before you are caught by surprise with unexpected weather for a longer period.

Okay, you have figured out your refrigeration, batteries, anchor tackle, sailing gear and hopefully your engine as well.

The next really big systems to test and understand are the electronic navigation tools. As we mentioned previously, you can easily have what we call electronic navigation aided groundings or collisions if you do not practice using these tools. The electronics, as well as your autopilot, are the keys to safe, happy, cruising for couples.

We strongly recommend you have an old fashioned paper chart to compare with your navigation system and practice using them together. Check to see what range the chartplotter is on before dangerous details disappear from your screen. If you are not already experienced navigators, plan on taking a course on navigation. It goes back to map reading skills. If you know how to read a map, then when you use Google maps and your automotive navigation in your car, you understand the directions. You should know how to read a nautical chart, so that you understand what you are looking at on your chartplotter. By taking time to practice using the chartplotter and making note of what range your navigation tools need to be set on, you can be comfortable that your chartplotter is giving you reasonably accurate position.

You should also practice using the autopilot. Test to see how well it holds a course and if it has other useful features, like auto tack, or if linked to the wind indicator, see if it can hold you into the wind for hoisting sails. It is an excellent tool for short handed sailing, as it frees you both for handling the sails. The autopilot is your most valuable crewmember. It doesn't eat, just maybe drinks a little hydraulic fluid every now and then, so make sure you know how to feed it fluids.

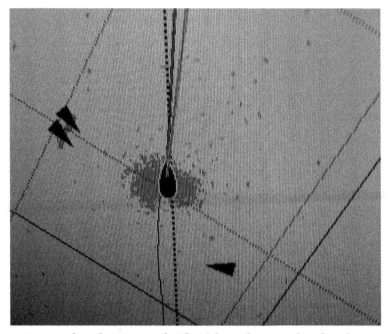

Example of AIS overlaid with radar on the display.

If you have an AIS receiver, you will want to test this system as well. We recommend testing to see how far a range ships pop up on your display. Test the system by day at first and if possible, anchor off a shipping channel in shallow water and practice looking up the information about the ships.

Practice understanding "Closest Point of Approach" (CPA) and the "Time of Closest Point of Approach" (TCPA). In daylight you can see just how fast they are upon your position. Then, when anchored at night, you can practice seeing their night navigation lights before you are actually try to navigate around these behemoths.

Checklist to see if you are ready to go.

1. Refrigeration: locate cold spots in your refrigerator/freezer and good produce storage.

2. Batteries: test how long they stay charged and how long they take to recharge and verify if you have enough battery capacity and charging sources.

3. Anchoring system: test windlass, check marking, length of chain and snubber, as well as ease to prepare to deploy, retrieve and stow for sea.

4. Sailing systems: check standing and running rigging, furling gear, deck hardware, winches, proper labeling of clutches, etc.

5. Navigation tools: practice use of chartplotter, depth sounder, wind instruments, etc.

6. Practice use of the autopilot; check to see how the flux gate compass on the autopilot control head reads in comparison to the chartplotter and the binnacle compass; test system use and find out what maintenance is needed.

7. If equipped with AIS, test range and practice using CPA and TCPA, as well as reading details about the ships and how to call them by name.

8. Conduct heavy weather practice near homeport for short periods.

9. Discuss emergency scenarios and what to do if something goes wrong.

10. Have fun on short trips, to gain confidence before venturing long distances.

Adding Equipment

After you have spent a few weeks to months actually using the boat, you have a better idea of what items you really need to add. It is time to break out that shopping list and break it into three parts. First, determine what items you really must have to make basic operation of the boat manageable for just two, or which items relate to safety equipment. Second, put on the list things you want to add to the boat. Finally, list the things you would like to have installed if you have enough money left (nice-to-haves). Then get out that West Marine or Defender catalog and start pricing out parts; this will give you an idea of dollar amounts to budget for these additions. If you can install what ever it is, great; if you have to pay someone to install it, well, take the cost of parts and double it, to give you a ballpark idea of budget.

The next step is finding a vendor to perform the work, and please, do not hire the first guy you talk to. The following steps will give you a guide on how to go about asking the right questions.

How to select Vendors to work on your boat.

In the marine industry, more so than any other industry, one needs to be very careful in selecting vendors to work on your boat. There are many outstanding vendors in the marine industry; however, sadly, there are many really bad vendors in the marine industry. How do you tell the difference?

1. Get recommendations from trusted sources, preferably sources that have used those vendors recently and had a good experience. Also, make sure the person referring the source knows what your "style" is. Some people seek the lowest cost no matter what it looks like when the job is done. For some, cost is no object, but they want high quality work and the best components. Most of us are somewhere in between. But if you ask the "dock rat" on the boat next to you for a recommendation and don't qualify it, he'll recommend from his own perspective.

2. Get references. Make sure these are up to date.

3. <u>Always</u> ask what their rates are, how they charge and what their payment policies are <u>before</u> any work starts. <u>Never</u> make the final payment until you are 100% satisfied with the work. Always obtain a quote, or at least an estimate for the work, <u>before</u> they start. There are some jobs, especially those requiring diagnosis of a problem and those requiring pulling wires and hoses, that are harder to estimate due to unknowns with your particular boat. However, if they are truly experienced in their field, they will at least be able to give you ball park idea.

4. For major purchases, like a new suit of sails or a whole new electronics suite, consider creating a Request for Bids (Proposals) that gives enough information for them to provide an accurate quote, and send this to at least three companies.

5. Schedule. Cheops Law (ancient Egyptian Pharaoh who built some of the pyramids): "Nothing ever gets built on time, on budget." In all our decades of boating we've worked with only one yard in Florida that completes their quoted work on time/on budget, every time. We're sure there are other yards in Florida every bit as good, but we just haven't looked for them once we found the one we're happy with in our area. A common occurrence with a not so good yard goes like this: "We need a bottom job and a couple other things done (work that should take about one week). When can we bring her in?" Yard: "Bring in her in tomorrow." In she goes, hauled and blocked in the yard, and there she sits. A week later no work has started. A week after that, enough work has started that you can't re-launch her. Now you're calling every other day. And, guess what, they find all sorts of other work that just must be done on your boat before she can be launched. Four to six weeks later, and with twice the amount of dollars you expected, you get your boat back, often with only adequate work quality.

IN THE MARINE BUSINESS, THE LOWEST COST BIDDER IS ALMOST NEVER THE BEST VALUE CHOICE!!! You *will* end up paying more in the long run.

The yard we love isn't the cheapest by any means, but they aren't expensive either. They are, for us, the best value, since they carefully schedule their work. We call for a bottom job and they say "We can fit you in six weeks from now." We show up on the appointed day, they haul, do the work, and have her back at the end of the week.

6. Vendor chasing. "When can you start?" "On Monday" Monday comes and no show and no phone call. On Tuesday, you call and ask what happened, "Oh, had an emergency call from another boat, will get to you tomorrow." No show or call on Wednesday either, but Thursday, he's there tearing into things aboard. It's a job that should take two days. Friday, he is a no show and does not answer your phone calls. The next Tuesday, he returns and notes that parts were missing and, oh by the way, it'll take twice as long because the "whatamacallit," is screwed up. We once were going on a two-week vacation and wanted to use our boat as soon as we got home. There were three projects we wanted done, all of which would take the boat out of service. We contracted three vendors to do the jobs and told them our two-week schedule. Only one vendor had the work done upon our return. The other two had started their jobs on the last day of the two weeks, so that we were unable to use the boat when we got home. We've learned to never tell the vendor the last day you really need to have the job done. Back it up at least a week. Sometimes the delay isn't the vendor's fault; it's a boat, and it is not unusual for something to crop up in the middle of a project that will delay the finish date.

Example 1: *We had an outstanding electronics technician who was the only guy we'd let touch electronic or electrical systems on our boat. After a lightning strike, we contracted with the company he worked for to do the insurance covered work. A week later the technician left to start up his own company, (the tech couldn't warn us for contractual reasons) and they sent "dumb & dumber" to do the work. We eventually realized we had to check their work every day to catch the mistakes; for example, we found an improperly installed inverter using wire nuts, a hard turn on a sharp fresh cut fiberglass corner with a thin sensor wire, and we had a hard time getting some of the electronics to talk properly. It also took forever to complete the work.*

Several years later, we were hit again by lightning. This time, we made sure our outstanding guy did the work. It was completed on time, on budget and the quality of the installation and wiring was a work of art! Both companies charged the same rates.

Example 2: *A company with a good reputation installed three air-conditioning systems. Overall, the company did a good job, but installed three new thru hulls for cooling water outlets, each about three inches above resting waterline with plastic thru hulls and no seacocks! When challenged, they said, "Well, they're above the waterline." To which we replied, "Sailboat! These thru hulls will be below the heeled waterline!" The thru hulls were replaced with the proper material with ball valve seacocks on each.*

7. ABYC certification and other applicable standards: Yacht building and repair is a self-regulated industry with the American Boat & Yacht Council (ABYC) providing the recommendations for all aspects of yacht construction and proper maintenance/repair. Note, these are recommendations only; there are few laws regulating the industry.

However, the ABYC standards have become so accepted that no major boat builder can risk the liability of not conforming to them. In fact, most of the major builders are actively involved in ABYC helping to raise the quality and safety of all of their fleets. With vendors though, it's a very different story. The ABYC offers a set of certifications covering all of the major fields of boat maintenance and repair. For example: Electrical systems, Machinery, General Systems, Corrosion. The good vendors take the time to attend the ABYC courses for their field and get the certifications that keep them current in their field with continuing education. Look for vendors that are ABYC certified; it shows they take a professional approach and pride in their work and that they are trained to the proper standards. When you go to sell your boat, the surveyor will be trained in ABYC standards and will note any work that does not meet the standards, which may affect your sale price.

8. Are the vendors boaters? Do they ever actually use the equipment they install or work on? The vendor we swear by for air conditioning and refrigeration work is professionally trained and ABYC certified, and owns a cruising boat with systems and *actually cruises it*. He knows what really works out there and what doesn't. Many times, we've gotten on a boat that has a new electronics package and it's clear right from power up that the installer isn't a sailor (or at least not one who actually goes cruising). The physical installation may have been done properly, but none of the commissioning and sea trial settings have been touched, nor have some of the proper interfacing between units, like the autopilot and other systems, been completed.

9. Have they worked on a system just like yours? There is not a lot of standardization in marine systems. Each product will have its own proprietary interfaces and idiosyncrasies. Does your vendor know these for your system?

10. If it's a big job, make sure you get progress updates on a regular basis. The good vendors provide a lot of communication, keeping you up to date on the status, plans, schedule and cost incurred to date.

Some repairs may require climbing the mast.

Don't forget to ask if the electronics technician will go up the mast or if you need to hire a rigger to go up.

STEP 4 - Checklist

1. Get organized, check your inventory,
Make a place for everything and put everything in its place.

2. Check your safety gear, fire extinguishers, flares and first aid kit. Make sure you comply with USCG regulations for your size vessel.

3. Create a maintenance list

4. Register your VHF radio; make sure it is connected to the GPS and enter your MMSI#.

5. Register your EPIRB with your emergency contact information.

6. Get an FCC Radio/Radar license if you are planning international travel.

7. Find the good marine vendors in your area mechanics, electricians, etc.

8. Live at anchor for at least one week disconnected from shore power to test battery life and charging systems.

9. Create a formal Log.

10. Practice night sailing and return to homeport; practice heavy weather sailing.

Resources you may find helpful.

Know Your Boat: The Guide to Everything that Makes Your Boat Work. by David Kroenke

Boatowner's Mechanical and Electrical Manual: How to Maintain, Repair and Improve Your Boat's Essential Systems by Nigel Calder

Trouble Shooting Marine Diesels by Peter Compton

The Sailmaker's Apprentice: A Guide for the Self-Reliant Sailor, by Marino Emilano

The Complete Rigger's Apprentice: Tools and Technique for Modern and Traditional Rigging. by Brion Toss

The Annapolis Book of Seamanship, by John Rousmaniere

Magazines and Websites:

Blue Water Sailing www.bwsailing.com

Cruising World www.cruisingworld.com

Cruising Outpost www.cruisingoutpost.com

Ocean Navigator www.oceannavigator.com

Practical Sailor www.practicalsailor.com

SAIL Magazine www.sailmagazine.com

Defender Industries www.defender.com

West Marine www.westmarine.com

Step 5

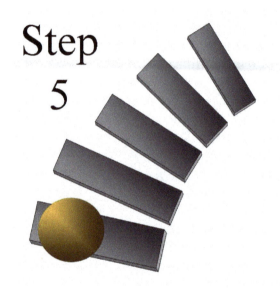

Get Advanced Training

STEP 5 Get Advanced training

The additional training you need now that you own a boat.

After you have bought your cruising boat, it is a good idea to dial in on any gaps in your experience or education. Some training is very specific to your boat and equipment; for example, not all boats come with radar or a Single Side Band (SSB) radio. If your boat is equipped with radar you are required by law to know and understand how to navigate using radar and will be held liable for any incident that could have been avoided using this valuable tool. Having a boat equipped with SSB can provide you with long range communications and inexpensive access to the Internet with the addition of a Pactor Modem. This tool is not plug and play, so you need to give yourself time to learn how it works and proper tuning.

We recommend Marty Brown's book *Marine SSB for Idi-Yacht's,* an excellent step-by-step guide to understanding your single side band and (HF) High Frequency radio systems.

In addition, the SSB gives you a means to gather weather data from the National Weather Service in the form of wind and wave forecast faxes, which are broadcast at no charge several times a day. We also want to recommend that you take a formal navigation class and continue with advanced navigation training. These navigation courses are challenging and should be an excellent foundation for the inexperienced and help keep you safe.

Lastly, but most important, is learning how to read and understand the weather forecast. You need to know how and where to get the data you need to decide when to begin a voyage. The single factor that effects your enjoyment of the cruising lifestyle is the weather. Weather can provide the most drama and ruin your dream in just one wrong outing. Making a bad judgment call could end your partnership, or worst case, end with you having to abandon your boat at sea and risking others' lives to save you. In our opinion, the most important and valuable training you can get is how to understand the weather.

We have made two short checklists for navigation and weather for you to see how your knowledge stacks up. If you cannot check off any of the boxes on the checklist, make sure you schedule a course.

Sean & Cynthia "Arkuda" Privilege 495 Catamaran
Studying Advanced Navigation

Why you need Navigation training.

Many people these days take navigation for granted. After all, we no longer bother to use a map. Just type in the address to our GPS automobile navigation tool and the little voice coming from the dash board tells us to turn right in 1.3 miles. So why do we need to know how to read a nautical chart? There will be a chartplotter on board. Isn't that the same thing as my iPhone navigation app? Well, the answer is yes and no. In fact, we recommend that clients use either iNavX or the Navionics apps on their devices like iPhone, iPad or Android as a back up to the ship's navigation tools.

On many of our offshore training voyages with couples, one third (yes, 33 percent) of the time the electronic navigation system had some type of failure.

Here are just a few examples of what could go wrong. Once, the GPS antenna connection was bad, so the chartplotter did not have the position of the boat. Another time, the chartplotter LED screen backlight went out and was just black, so it could not be read. Then there was the time we were struck by lightening so everything went black.

It would be prudent for both of you to know how to navigate the old fashioned way with a good old paper chart. The paper chart is sunlight readable, requires no power, is instant on and the screen size is usually about 17.5" X 24", in the form of a chart kit. Some chart kits will provide you with the ability to determine your course in either True or Magnetic. However, some only come with a compass rose in True, so you will need to have an understanding of deviation, variation and how to convert your course from True to Magnetic to Compass to calculate your course to steer.

We suggest you take the ASA 105 navigation course. It will be a challenge for most, but a worthwhile exercise. There are also navigation courses put on by your local Power Squadron as well as online courses you can take when it's either too cold or too hot for sailing. Even if you take the course and do not understand it completely, you will get the basics.

Pictured above is Jeff returning from skippering his first Gulf Stream crossing to the Bahamas in the 70's

What about navigating in current, crossing the Gulf Stream or the Loop current when crossing the Gulf of Mexico?

If you were planning on popping over to the Bahamas, you will encountering the largest river in the world called the Gulf Stream. Even if you are sailing from the West Coast of Florida to the Yucatan Peninsula in Mexico, you will encounter the Gulf Stream in the form of the Loop Current. Did you know that this affects sailing across the Gulf of Mexico as far north as Mississippi? We want you to recognize there is more to learn than how that GPS chartplotter works.

They said "It's not rocket science" but....

Example: *We were on the dock at a marina and a couple was looking for a place to stay. They had bought a 33' boat, moved aboard and taken off sailing along the Florida West Coast. "This isn't rocket science" he said, "We'll figure it out as we go." While figuring things out, they had an adventure while trying to transit an unmarked pass. They did not know to check local knowledge on this pass. If they had, they would have learned that this pass has what some call "living sand," meaning the sand bars are constantly shifting. The couple tried the pass, using their chartplotter in weather they should not have been out in, and cut too close to the lee shore sand bar. When they lost engine power and grounded on the sand, they broke their keel and rudder. Though rescued, they soon became homeless while they waited for the boat to be repaired. They were lucky they did not lose the boat or their lives. By the way, we did note she was pregnant and they had three dogs aboard!*

Try placing the cover over the chartplotter. Look around at where the land ends, where the channel markers or other reference points are, and then mark your position on the chart. Take the cover off the chartplotter and see how close you came to your actual position. We call this the "where are we now game," show me on the chart.

Note: Read the disclaimer displayed when the chartplotter is powered up: "Not to be used as a single source for navigation. Not a replacement for government charts." Every chartplotter on the market displays a similar message.

Navigation class under a coconut palm.

Navigation skills checklist

1. You can navigate with a paper chart, parallel rules and dividers.

2. You know how to use a hand-bearing compass and take a fix.

3. You understand how to read tide and current tables.

4. You know the "Rules of the Road," both inland and international.

5. You can determine a course to steer to account for leeway and for current set and drift.

6. You know how to dead reckon and plot your position on a chart.

7. You can pilot a boat in an unfamiliar harbor.

8. You can navigate without the use of a chartplotter.

9. You know how to plan a voyage to arrive in daylight hours.

10. You know not to enter an unfamiliar harbor at night.

Cindy and Ron "Storm Walker" MacGregor 26

Why you want to learn more about how to interpret weather, radar and Single Side Band.

Weather forecasting has improved immensely over the last thirty years. We used to call the VHF weather channel the "comedy channel," because it was often way off the mark. Now, the weather channel is much, much, better although there are still a few days when one wonders if the weathermen have bothered to look out the window. Here are two examples of the importance of understanding the weather. Keep in mind, both of these examples involve experienced sailors with skills in offshore heavy weather wind and seas.

Example 1: *Back in 1983, Jeff owned a Cal 25 named "Zoo" and sailed it mostly on Tampa Bay. Our friend, Steve, owned a Nouveau 27, named "Evoleno" ("One love" spelled backwards) and lived aboard with his wife Becky and two kittens. We decided to sail together in consort to the Dry Tortugas. We cruised down the Florida West Coast to Captiva Island and anchored off the north side of Red Fish Pass to await a weather window for the 140 nautical miles passage to the Tortugas. When the forecast called for 10-15 knots from the east with 3 - 4 foot seas, setting us up for a perfect beam reach, we set off under full sail and timed our exit for an overnight run with arrival at daylight. As the day went on, the wind continued to build, and both boats shortened sail in sync with each rise of the wind speed. The seas built with the wind and just before sunset, we took a photograph from Zoo that showed just the tip of Evoleno's mast sticking up above the wave between us. (Think how big the waves were when only the tip of the mast could be seen.)*

By sunset, we each had only our storm jibs up, the smallest sails we had aboard, and were still reaching at full speed. We would take two waves up, turning our bows into the wind so we didn't take the big rollers on the beam. By steering the boat this way, we walked over the waves in an S shaped path as they passed under us. Then, we'd take one wave downwind, surfing off with accelerating, keel humming speed. Two up and one down and we averaged out on our course. Remember that in those days, our only navigation was Radio Direction Finding on the tower on Logger Head Key in the Tortugas. This actually worked quite well. The tower gave us bearing and since the bottom slopes up steadily our depth sounder gave us range.

You could only see the tip of the mast above the waves.

As night fell, the winds peaked up to 40 knots, with some of the waves breaking over our flush deck Cal 25. Jeff's crew, Bill, asked how we were going to see the waves to steer up and down them in the dark. Although it was howling, it was a clear night and Jeff just smiled and said, "You'll see them!" As a big roller approached, it would blot out the stars and sound like a small train approaching. So it was up two and down one all night.

Meanwhile, the VHF weather channel continued to describe 10-15kn and 3-4' seas in Florida Bay where we were. That night we weren't laughing at the irony. By morning, the winds and seas had backed down and we finished our approach to the Tortugas with a fine reach and had a splendid time there.

Example 2: *Fast forward thirty years later. We are doing on board Voyage Training, working with Jack and Jill sailing their Hunter 50cc from Florida to St. Thomas, USVI. We have Sirius satellite weather on board. We have just downloaded an updated set of 24, 48, and 72-hour weather charts from NOAA, before we set off for a 36-hour offshore passage from Great Exuma to Provodenciales (Provo) in the Turks and Caicos. The forecast and our own weather eyes call for calm weather for the first third of the trip and beam winds northeast at 10 knots for the second third, with the wind shifting to the east and building to 15 knots during the last third. The first third was spot on and we made our way east while the northeast wind started up. But the shift in the wind to the east happened early and then went a bit south to ESE and soon we were motor sailing to the SE.*

Before noon on the second day, the wind climbed to 15 knots, as forecast, but it didn't stop there. It kept building until we had a steady 30 knots, with peak gusts to 35 knots (41.4 knots apparent wind per our recording wind gauge). With the Atlantic open to Africa before us, the seas built and soon we were no longer motor sailing but doing what we call "motor slamming." The waves came from different angles across a range of about 50 degrees, so we spent the rest of the day in a windy washing machine until we could fetch the lee of Provo and find a nice peaceful anchorage there. Through all this, Sirius weather still showed the wind (where we were) as east at 15 knots versus the 30+ from the southeast that we experienced.

In the first example, decades ago, the weather forecasting was not that accurate, so no matter what the forecast, you had to have the skills to endure whatever the wind and sea conditions threw at you. Today, with the technology that is available and the quality of the forecasting, you can time your passages to avoid having to sail in heavy weather. If you time it right and take short hops you can eliminate the drama stories.

However, if you plan on making passages in open water lasting more than three days, you must be prepared to sail in heavy weather up to and including hurricane force winds. The lesson learned is that you must get the best forecast you can, compare all the weather sources you can, then secure for the worst and hope for the best!

The key to enjoying the cruising life is your ability to understand the weather and forecasting. If possible, *wait* for the right weather window to go. If you know the weather will close in, you can make plan B for where you want to land if you cannot make it as far as your plan A. Make a plan C if you know bad weather is coming. Be prepared and you will survive it.

So you have taken our advice on choosing the right weather window to make short passages; don't stop paying attention to the weather. Here is one more example of why you need to invest in a simple ship's barometer and why you shouldn't let your guard down just because you are happily cruising along, one little hop at a time.

The Barometer is a key tool for weather prediction.

Learn how to use the barometer and watch the sky for changing clouds. Through practice comes understanding, when it comes to reading the clouds. You should be able to see the wind on the water in the form of white caps, but often, people miss the bigger warning signs far in advance. By practicing observing the clouds each and every day, you can learn to relate the changing patterns to the oncoming weather. While you're still tied to shore, listen to the forecast, look at the clouds, watch the change, and before you know it, you will see the weather coming.

Buy an old fashioned barometer, where you set the needle to line up, and monitor the drop or rise in pressure. This is an incredibly simple tool that every boat should have aboard. The following story will illustrate how this will help you see the weather before it arrives. A storm should never come from nowhere.

Example of a Barometer (Weems and Plath)

Knowing when to watch out:

One evening, while cruising in the Bahamas, we tapped on the Barometer and the needle went down with a thump. The Barometer's reading of 1009mb was the lowest reading we had seen so far this trip, and it was our first clue that we were not going to get a full night's sleep.

We had spent the day beating our way into strong easterly trade winds, sailing the 50 nautical miles from Plana Cay to Mayaguana in the company of a 55' Tri and a Pearson 36'. We arrived late afternoon and dropped the hook in 15' of water. Though the anchor held when we backed down with the usual 2/3rds cruising power, Jeff still put on his snorkel gear and went to check on it. It was a good thing, too, since our 66lb Bruce anchor was nicely caught on a big rock. The Tri and the Pearson joined us and, since Jeff was already wet, he checked their anchors as well. They were also hung on rocks. There was nothing but rocks around and astern of our trio. On most of these Out Islands, there is a wall that drops off to no soundings. Off our bow, only about 100yds to the east, lay a very ugly set of shallow rocks and reef.

Normally, we would never consider staying hooked on a big rock overnight, but the weather was clear and fine and there was nothing of concern in the forecast, weather charts, or on radar. The east trade winds had been blowing steadily for days and if we dragged anchor, we had about 50 nautical miles to the west before we hit anything. It should blow light out of the east all night, like it had for the last several nights. In light conditions like these, just the weight of the anchor and 100' of chain would keep us in place. There were also no other protected places that we could reach before nightfall that would have allowed us to anchor in good sand.

Our friends on the Pearson invited us over for dinner, and though we've been sailing in consort with them for four days, this was our first chance to meet them in person! It was just before heading over to their boat, around 1900, (7pm) when we tapped the Barometer and saw the needle fall. We checked our weather sources again and there were no signs of trouble. On deck, it was a crystal clear star filled night, yet we made a mental note to keep a sharp weather eye out.

We returned from a great dinner at our neighbors and noticed to the west, in the far distance, flashes of light across the whole sky. We'd seen this look before in Florida when the East and West Coast sea breezes collide in the middle of the state. Based on this, Jeff estimated the distance of the storm at 80 nautical miles. A check of the ship's radar on a range set out to 50 nautical miles showed all clear. We decided to get up in a few hours to check on the weather.

At 1:30 am, we rolled over in our berth and heard that muted distant thunder that one can only hear when it is very quiet. A check outside revealed lightning all the way across the western horizon, and a check of the radar showed a solid storm line at about 40 miles. Jeff set his stopwatch to 6 minutes to calculate its speed and quickly realized that the watch wasn't needed. The storm line was moving so fast that we could almost see it moving on the screen and a quick calculation showed it would be over us in less than 90 minutes. When a storm line is moving this fast, it usually means it will be very intense. The strong west wind that was sure to be in this storm would put us on the rocks in seconds. We needed to head out to sea!

This is one of the reasons that we always kept Polyphonic *ready for sea. Even when we had the anchor set in good holding, and planned to be there a long time, she was kept stowed and ready to run on short notice. As we were preparing to leave, we noticed our friends on the Tri were also up and clearing away for leaving. They hailed us and asked if we thought a half a mile offshore was enough sea room.*

We told them we were going for 3 miles. We wanted room to sail around Mayaguana's southwest corner in case of engine failure. Meanwhile, there was no sign of life on the Pearson. The captain and crew were experienced lake racers, but they were new to cruising and had just bought the Pearson in Ft. Lauderdale a month earlier. Hails on the VHF got no answer, so Jean got the spotlight and flashed it in their ports until we got a hail, "Are you signaling us?" We told them about the storm, and they asked, "What do you think we should do?" and we replied, "We can't tell you what to do, but Polyphonic and the Tri are heading out to sea right now!" They were quickly on deck and headed out with us. Sure enough, just as we started to motor out to sea, the first drizzle of rain started.

We got our sea room as the wind almost instantly jumped to a sustained 35 knots+ with frequent gusts deep into the 50-knot range, with very heavy rain and a lot of lightning. Fortunately, the underlying sea was calm, and the storm line was moving too fast for significant waves to develop. If we had been asleep when the storm hit, we would have been on the reef before we had time to react.

We could clearly see the storm front on the radar and were able to pick a weak point to pass through. We could also see the backside of the line, and thus had an idea of just how long it would take for the storm to pass over us. About an hour later it was all over, with clear skies and bright stars shining again. All three boats turned back and headed for our next day's destination, Abraham Bay on the south side of Mayaguana.

For us, with a lot of night sailing and thunderstorm experience, and the radar to see what was coming, it was business as usual. In fact, we took turns napping during the storm. For our friends on the Pearson, it was a bit terrifying. It was only their third night ever spent at sea and the first in a storm. We enjoyed the cruising company of the Pearson all the way to Guadeloupe. They have remained in the Caribbean and are now quite seasoned cruisers.

Lessons Learned:

1. Even when the weather is clear and forecast to remain so, keep your weather eye out, especially when you are not comfortable with the anchorage. This storm was not a cold front, tropical wave, or any other forecast or long-term system that could be planned for or tracked.

2. Gain the experience of sailing at night and of sailing in storms before you leave.

3. Dive on your anchor. We had backed ours down to our usual "well set" rpm and it held fine. But in this case it would have only held for easterly winds and would have tripped free for most other wind directions.

4. Have a plan to run out to sea.

5. Get sea room while you can.

6. Use Radar to track the weather. Radar is a fantastic and underestimated tool for tracking the weather. We met one cruiser who snuffed at radar saying, "I don't sail in the fog." We almost never have fog in our cruising grounds either, but we won't go offshore without radar any more.

7. When sailing in heavy wind and sea, always consider what to do if something goes wrong. Make a plan and then you will know what you need to do.

Test your Weather knowledge with this checklist

1. You can read the clouds

2. You can see the wind on the water.

3. You know how to use the ship's barometer.

4. You have listened to the VHF for weather.

5. You have a basic understanding of wind & wave weather forecast (available through the internet, near shore & via SSB offshore)

6. You have developed heavy weather sailing skills.

7. You can make a voyage plan based on the weather.

8. You have learned to make alternate plans if the weather changes.

9. You are in the habit of securing the vessel for sea under any conditions.

10. You have practiced forecasting the weather using multiple sources and verified the outcome.

STEP 5 Checklist

1. You have both attended a "Safety at Sea" seminar.

2. You both know how to navigate with your chartplotter.

3. You have a general understanding of how to obtain information on the weather, or have hired a weather routing service before making a passage.

4. You have tested out all your boat systems and have a basic understanding of how to repair vital systems, like the engine and head.

5. If your boat is equipped with radar, you have taken courses in how it operates, tuning and interpretation of your equipment.

6. If your boat is equipped with Single Side Band, you have practiced using this long range communication.

7. If your boat is equipped with solar panels, you understand how the system is connected to your charging source.

8. If your boat is equipped with a wind generator you understand how to operate it and secure it for high winds.

9. If your boat is equipped with a watermaker, you have practiced making water and cleaning the filters.

10. You have purchased charts and cruising guides to the area you plan to cruise.

Resources

The Annapolis School of Seamanship
www.annapolisschoolofseamanship.com

The American Sailing Association Courses
www.ASA.com

Steve & Doris Colgate's Offshore Sailing School
www.offshore-sailing.com

U.S. Sailing – Safety At Sea seminar
www.ussailing.org

American Boat and Yacht Council (ABYC)
www.ABYCinc.org

Mack Boring Diesel Engine Owner Training
www.MackBoring.com

Lee Chesneau Marine Weather Courses
www.weatherbylee.com

Chris Parker Marine Weather Center
https://mwxc.com

Radar for Mariners
by David Burch

Play time!

Fun with new friends!

Example of a couples first Voyage with "Two Can Sail"

Say you bought a boat in Florida and you live in the Annapolis area and you plan to move the boat closer to home. Many of you are thinking, "Why would we go through all that stuff and make an inventory now; we'll do it when we get the boat home." We have found that many of our training voyages require an offshore passage, and if you want to keep the drama out of the dream, knowing what you have on board is critical.

We strive for "All Dream and No Drama" on our voyage training with you and your new boat. It will take at least two days to get ready! We know you are excited and very eager to get going and likely have a window of time off from work that you have to complete the voyage by a certain number of days. No matter what your schedule, it is critical to remember that it *will* take at least two days to get the boat ready for the trip, so plan accordingly.

If getting the boat from A to B quickly is your only goal, put the boat on a truck. The cost is about the same, it saves wear and tear on the boat and is much faster. You can also hire a pure delivery skipper, and he'll get her home "hell or high water", usually in one piece. But if you both want to learn your boat and get real cruising experience on the way, then factor in the extra time needed. Brand new boats are not exempt from this. In fact, sometimes they can take longer, because they have none of the items aboard needed for actually living on the boat.

All of the couples that have hired us for voyage training have trusted us when we note it will take at least two days to get ready for the voyage home. But they are always scratching their heads thinking they've just bought a boat that was supposed to be "ready to go."

This is an old adage: "Stuff always expands to exceed available space, independent of how much space is available." We've often done the survey and found the vessel sound and seaworthy, but there are additional things that we do that take the two plus days. Most of the time, the boat has been sailed and maintained by the guy. Our experience is that most guys are just not great organizers, and it is the woman who makes the home. We find stuff shoved in every drawer, locker, hold and compartment aboard with no room for you to put your things. It's often a lot of good stuff mixed with a lot of junk. So, the first thing is to empty everything out, inventory it, decide what is useful to keep, useful to sell or give away, and what should be thrown away. Eliminate as much packaging and volume as possible. Then, re-stow everything in locations that make sense to you and are stowed from a safety perspective.

While the boat is empty, this is the time to clean all those lockers and holds. "We can do all that when we get the boat home," you are thinking. To have a safe voyage, you need to have a place for everything and everything in its place. Often times, the boat has only been sailed near the coast and the voyage home will require some offshore work, which requires a different level of stowing and securing gear. Also, why not start your trip home in a nice clean boat instead of sailing home with all the dirt, grime and maybe even bugs aboard! We can usually complete this step in half a day, depending on the boat size and how much stuff is aboard.

Now that the inventory is done, you'll know what you need to purchase from the marine supply store to fill out the mandatory equipment list.

If you're planning to only coastal cruise when you get home, investing in offshore safety gear wouldn't make sense right now. If you sail with us, we provide our own $8,000 package of offshore safety equipment, which includes a 6 person Winslow life raft, offshore SOLAS flares, fully equipped Rapid Ditch Bag, Iridium Sat phone and more, which can save you from having to invest in this equipment at this stage.

There is usually a short project list, either from the survey or because you purchased a brand-new boat and are creating your own project list. Project lists usually require at least one more trip to the marine supply store.

You will also need to make a menu plan, create a provisions list, and then go shopping. This usually involves a trip to the grocery store and several carts worth of supplies. Our next book *Tips from Two Can Sail,* will include Jean's "Magic Prep" suggestions.

Do not underestimate the physical demands of spending 8-10 hours climbing on and off the boat, and up and down the companionway, carrying loads of equipment, gear, crates of food and sometimes things like anchors and chain. It's almost always dinner and then bed on that first day.

The second day is spent finishing any left over tasks and addressing new ones discovered on the first day. Then, it's time for serious planning. The charts and cruising guides are brought out and the route home studied in detail. Best case, worst case, and most likely route scenarios are discussed. Key waypoints and any danger areas are noted.

All of the available weather resources are then examined to see the long term and short term weather systems that will affect the trip. The first few days, plans are laid out in detail based on these weather forecasts.

Next, safety and emergency plans are worked out for the specific boat. What will we do in case of fire, sinking and medical emergencies? Ideally, these plans are written down and placed in a book that stays with the boat.

Finally, the boat is rigged for the trip with MOB lights, jacklines run, inflatable Personal Floatation Devices and harnesses tried on for fit and placed in the boat for easy access, the ship's log readied and placed at the navigation (nav) station, and watch schedules worked out and posted at the nav station. All of these steps are completed, even if the majority of the trip will be near the coast. If you are interested in getting your new boat home quickly, this usually means going offshore whenever the weather allows. Again, the best case, worst case, and most likely route scenarios are discussed. Then we get a good night's sleep before setting off.

Expect something to go wrong, or something to break, on your first voyage. If the vessel had a good survey, it should be something minor. Expect the unexpected! Even if you are just going around the state of Florida from the East Coast to the West Coast, you will cover almost the same distance as the trip from Florida to the Chesapeake. Welcome to cruising!

The next few pages include examples of a crew checklist of what items to bring and not to bring, a report of a Miami Boat Show delivery based on the log sheets, and a menu planning example, etc. You may find these helpful in planning your first voyage. Most couples are overwelmed with all the new systems and getting to know their new boat. You can use these checklists to provide information for friends or family that you plan on having as volunteer crew.

We also recommend you review these examples of a Mayday VHF call and what to do in case of an emergency requiring abandon ship or even a man over board situation with your crew prior to departure.

Vessel Name
Doc#1123456
Radio call letters: WCY 3456

Crew Gear List

Only One Bag Per Person *(plus your harness& Foul weather gear)*
 This is because we are a crew of six and all gear must be stowed somewhere (not on a berth) since trip involves overnights. Please be considerate of your crewmates and keep the bags to a minimum. Thanks

Required Items:
Photo ID
Inflatable PFD, with integral safety harness, with your name on it and a 6 FT lanyard with clip.
Whistle on the PFD
Personal strobe on the PFD
Foul weather gear
Seasick prevention medicine
Sunscreen lotion
Any personal medication required
Pocket flashlight (ideally with red mode for night use)
Sleeping Bag or bedding and pillow

Suggested Items:
Tripak of small Sky Flares (for pocket of foul weather jacket)
Rigging knife (for pocket)
Calymat (glow) sticks
Sailing gloves

Don't Bring:
Coolers, anything bulky that can't sit on the rail and trim sheets.

If you have and want to bring, please do:
GPS, Handheld VHF, Satellite Phone, Sextant

Crew Standing Orders & Boat Rules:

Doc#1123456
Radio call letters: WCY 3456
Owner: Jeff Grossman   Captain: Jean Levine

Standing Orders:

When in doubt, wake up the Skipper.
Wear your harness when on deck at night or when skipper asks.
Check bilge once every hour (feel free to check anytime you wish, the more the better)
Log position fix every two hours and at the change of watch. Also complete log, wind speed/direction, heading, weather and sea condition, which sails are flying. Boat speed and of course time in 24-hour time.
(Watch captains should plot position on chart before taking the next watch.)

Boat Rules (Please & Thank you)

ALWAYS put it (whatever it is) back EXACTLY where you got it, right after you use it.
   This is a safety issue. In an emergency Jeff and Jean know exactly where it is and it needs to be there!
If you don't know how to work it, DON'T try....ask someone who does.
You clog the head you clear the head no matter what the sea conditions.
(FYI the rebuild kit is now $175 for those cheesy plastic bits.)
Stow all gear, all the time, keep the floors clear.
   This is a safety issue. In an emergency we will need immediate access, especially to the engine room and the bilge access floorboards. We won't have time to be clearing clothes, gear, etc. sooo...please.

MAN OVER BOARD PROCEDURES

If you go over....MAKE A LOT OF NOISE!!!!
If you see someone go over........SCREAM "MAN OVER BOARD!!!!" And do not take your eyes off the person, even for a moment.
Helm.... If jib up, throw the wheel over....if chute up, note heading, hold steady course, get crew to sock chute FAST then turn around and sail reverse course.
Person closest to NAV station quickly hit GPS MOB button; if you can write down the position, even better, (we will have a handheld GPS in cockpit push MOB and hit NAV button)
Cockpit crew: person closest to Helm head for MOB light and deploy, others throw cockpit cushions or horseshoe ring.
Keep talk to a minimum so that we can listen for the person in the water.
Plan is to return and recover under SAIL....primary reasons are: it is quiet we will be able to hear the person, we won't worry about the prop. Jib will come down before recovery.

ABANDON SHIP PROCEDURES   STAY CALM!!!

DO NOT LEAVE THE BOAT UNTIL JEFF GIVES WORD OR YOUR ALREADY SWIMMING!!! PUT ON LIFEJACKETS!! USE A LINE TO TIE EVERYONE TOGETHER, Don't get separated. MAKE SURE SOMEONE HAS THE BUG OUT BAG! (Located in starboard cockpit locker with Lifejackets.)
Person closest to NAV station should begin transmitting on high power 25 Watts VHF the following message: MAYDAY, MAYDAY, MAYDAY
Position is...read coordinates from GPS next to VHF. Repeat Three times.
We are sinking...we are sinking...
Repeat message continually, press DSC red emergency distress button on VHF.
Those on deck stay on deck, prepare life raft......if time grab inflatable dingy from fore peak, pump and paddles in port cockpit locker. Anything else that floats like cushions....send up on deck.

Meal Planning – A well-fed crew is a happy crew!
Please circle your choices for each.

Breakfast: Yogurt (Fruit, Fat Free, Plain....what's your favorite) Croissant, Bagels, Donuts, Muffins, granola bar... what's your favorite? Scrambled eggbeater burrito with ? Cheese, salsa, turkey bacon, ham? Cold Cereal: Rice Krispies, shredded wheat, cocoa puffs, fruit loops? Fill in the blank.....
your favorite_____.
Coffee   Espresso   Tea   with cream/sugar/nutra sweet/lemon?
Orange Juice   Cranberry   Apple

Lunch: Bread choices   Rolls, Wraps, White, Wheat, Rye?
Fillings: Turkey/ Ham/ Roast Beef/ Pastrami/ Swiss/ Cheddar/ Provolone/ Munster? Peanut butter (smooth or crunchy) Jelly (Strawberry/grape) BBQ Chicken sandwich /Beef Taco's/
_____?

Condiments: Ketchup/ Mustard/ Mayo / Hot sauce & Salsa / Vinaigrette / Ranch / Parmesan / Pickles sweet or dill/ Olives black or green Other_____

Snacks: Doritos/ Fritos/ Regular chips/ Pretzels/ mixed nuts/ Raisins/ Dried fruit/ Oreos /Nutter Butters/ Choc Chip cookies/ Oatmeal Raisin Brownies/ Ice cream bites
(fill in the blank in case I missed something.
What is your favorite midnight watch snack? Shhh I won't tell!)
Assorted Fresh Fruit/ Veggies/ Hard Boiled eggs.

Dinner examples:
1. Sliced roasted chicken breast with seasoned rice in warm wraps.
2. Baked Pasta twists in tomato sauce with ricotta cheese and salad.
3. Chicken, turkey bacon, tomato, Swiss cheese pasta club salad
4. Vegetarian Chili
5. Thai seasoned fish with veggies and rice
Please **pick two** dinner choices...... this helps a lot!

Please tell me: If you have any food or other allergies
_____
I CAN'T LIVE WITHOUT_____
   I CAN'T EAT (Don't like) _____

Crew List

Name :_____

Address:_____

Telephone: _____

Emergency contact: _____

Medications / Allergy? _____

After the trip I am staying aboard? Sharing hotel? Sailing back?

_____

Name :_____

Address:_____

Telephone: _____

Emergency contact: _____

Medications / Allergy? _____

After the trip I am staying aboard? Sharing hotel? Sailing back?

_____

Name :_____

Address:_____

Telephone: _____

Emergency contact: _____

Medications / Allergy? _____

After the trip I am staying aboard? Sharing hotel? Sailing back?

_____

Name :_____

Address:_____

Telephone: _____

Emergency contact: _____

Medications / Allergy? _____

After the trip I am staying aboard? Sharing hotel? Sailing back?

_____
_____

Report from a Miami Boat Show Delivery

Capt. Jean Levine
Crew: First Mate James Jones, Michelle & John Smith, Peter & Barbara Taylor

Feb 5, 2014 Boat inspection and systems review with crew. Brought equipment and supplies to boat, provisioning. Safety, Emergency procedures, Standing orders, Route planning and Weather briefings with crew. Calibrated depth sounder to read Depth of Water. Noted Eng Hours and fuel, water and propane levels.

Feb 6, 2014
07:30 Tank gauge near Full. Eng Hours = 8.3. Filled (2) fuel jugs with 10 gallons of reserve fuel.
11:00 Depart Regatta Point Marina with Catalina 385 and ran with her to Miami. Weather clear and wind NE 12kn and building.
13:00 SW Channel Bell taking course for Venice Inlet. NW swell with winds NE 10-17kn and fading.
16:00 27°19.04 082°37.90 Motorsailing south along coast.
18:45 Venice: Crows Nest Marina Long Dock. Note: Met Catalina 440 "Suite Jolene" and Catalina 400 "Mile High Dream" at long dock. Eng hours = 15.0

Feb 7, 2014
08:00 Transferred 10gl from jugs to main tank Eng hours = 15.0 Refilled jugs at Venice Fuel dock.
09:00 Underway out Venice Inlet. Morning started foggy but quickly cleared.
12:00 26°52.36 082°23.72 Motor sailing south along coast. Noted steady drip from shaft stuffing box.
18:00 26°18.61 082°04.79 Motoring. Added 10gl from fuel jugs. Eng hours 22.5
22:00 25°56.67 081°49.77 Motoring. Partly cloudy night. Shaft still leaking, bilge pump keeping up.

Feb 8, 2014
00:00   25°45.54 081°42.42   *Off Cape Romano. Motoring in smooth water.*
06:00   25°15.82 081°17.51   *Off NW Cape Sable. Only vessel sighted over night was the 385!*
12:00   24°52.03 080°49.77   *Cleared Yacht Channel heading for Channel 5 bridge and Hawk Channel*
17:00   *Anchored off Rodriguez Key for night.*

Feb 9, 2014
07:00   *Up anchor and underway up Hawk Channel. Foggy morning, visibility about ¾ mile. No Wind.*
10:15   *Entered Bay from Hawk Channel via Angel Fish Creek following the 385.*
12:00   *Motoring up Biscayne Bay. Water crystal clear.*
15:00   *Crandon Park fuel dock. Filled main tank to Full. 22 gallons. Eng Hours = 53.8*
16:30   *Show docks. 'C' slips not open so docked for night in 'B' slips. Eng Hours = 55.3*
       Estimated fuel consumption: 0.9 gl/hr @ 2000rpm

Maintenance "punch list" items noted:
Only systems not used were; TV, GenSet
1)   Stuffing box had steady leak. Tightened at Miami docks and not leaking while sitting idle in slip.
2)   Bilge Pump keeps getting stuck ON. Float switch intermittent.
3)   Forward Head outlet hose leaking at bowl. Changed hose clamp to larger size and tightened to almost stop leak. Recommend double checking.
4)   Forward Stateroom headboard Velcro failed and board dropped (all the way forward).
5)   Static interference on helm VHF. Could not remove with squelch.

Samples of Couples out Cruising

Cyndee and Dan Catalina 350 "Alibi"

One of the most rewarding aspects of our work with couples is when they contact us after having completed a new "first" in their cruising. Sometimes, these are their first weekend sailing trips on their own and anchoring out for the night, and sometimes it is their first transatlantic passage.

We have a fleet of couples out cruising that began their journey just like you. We have been blessed with the knowledge that our little ducklings are never alone, no matter where in the world they are, as one of our past graduates is nearby. We take great pride in introducing couples with similar tastes in boat type and cruising styles and connect them via social media, blogs or email.

Many of our couples stay in touch with us throughout their cruising and we have fun emailing a note like this "While you are in Georgetown, watch for Robin and Chris on a Catalina 445 named Cerulean", then finding out the couples connected and cruised side by side for months. Often we have "Two Can Sailors", one year ahead, two years ahead or more, making that Gulf Stream crossing or heading up the ICW or making the passage south to the Caribbean.

Bob playing guitar in the cockpit while Beth watches as the sun sets.

(Note: The fact that all three of these examples are Catalinas is a combination of coincidence and the fact that Catalina is a very popular choice for coastal and Caribbean cruising.)

Example # 1.
Nora and Norm were both retired military and had purchased a Catalina 440 as their first sailboat. Norm was a Navy Commander, so he was just learning what to do with those big, flat, white sails. He already knew seamanship, navigation, rules of the road, etc. Nora, on the other hand, was an Air Force Colonel from Oklahoma whom we teased, because she was "wondering what that water stuff was all about."

After a few training sessions, they were feeling comfortable handling the 440, but had to put off their first solo trip due to distractions at home. A few months later, we were on a drive home from a voyage when Nora and Norm called from an anchorage on a Sunday morning, very proud of having navigated, sailed, and anchored successfully off the beautiful Emerson Point on Tampa Bay's Manatee River.

Example #2.
We helped Penny and Pete out when they purchased their brand new Catalina 445. They had both sailed in their younger years, but now, as retirement neared, they were ready to sail again. We knew they had become real cruisers when they sent an email to us, very excited about having just completed their first cruise from Florida to Charleston, South Carolina. The first thing they mentioned is that they had found a marina, that had nice showers and a laundromat.

The Catalina Fleet cruising together.

Example #3:
Olivia and Oscar weren't quite sure about taking on the cruising life style for their retirement. Like many couples we sail with, Oscar had much more experience, and was the driving force behind the idea. They attended one of our Couples Cruising Seminars, and both came away convinced they could do it. They followed our 5 Step Plan, getting sailing lessons, diesel lessons, and others, and worked on their sailing skills while they started researching boats. They narrowed it down to a Catalina 42, which we surveyed for them in Brunswick, Georgia on a 102° degree day. We then did boat orientation and voyage training with them, moving the boat from Brunswick, Georgia to Charleston, South Carolina.

Oscar & Olivia figured it would take at least six months to sell their home, so they planned to use that time to get to know the boat and to plan their move aboard. Their home sold in two weeks.

They hurriedly moved aboard after moving out of a house they had lived in for 42 years. We met them in Charleston shortly after the move, and they were still in a bit of shock from the much more rapid then expected transition.

After some time learning their boat and doing the modifications they had planned, they set sail up the East Coast for Maine.

Olivia was still getting used to the life style, and preferred to only do day voyaging, no overnight or offshore work. They worked their way up and back down the East Coast, running during the day only, until they were in South Florida. Oscar pointed out to Olivia that they could sail to Bimini in daylight, only 45 miles! Olivia said "I can do that," and over to Bimini they went, cruising the Bahamas all the way to the Out Islands. Oscar then said, "We can sail to the Dominican Republic with just one over night" and Olivia said, "I can do that", and off to the Dominican Republic they went.

Olivia told us later that at each stage, Oscar would just chart the next step and she could see that she could handle it until, the next thing she knew, they were in Trinidad!

Several years after Olivia & Oscar attended the Couples Cruising Seminar, they were invited to return as guests on our Couples Panel Discussion that we hold at the end of each Seminar. One of the women attendees asked Olivia, "When did you finally get over your anxieties, about voyaging?" Olivia answered: "I haven't yet! I've posted a sign in our Nav Station that says 'Life Begins at the End of Your Comfort Zone!' "

Olivia & Oscar have continued to enjoy the dream of the cruising life style, extensively sailing the Caribbean.

Push the edge of your comfort zone and follow these 5 Steps and you two can sail this dream!

Step 1

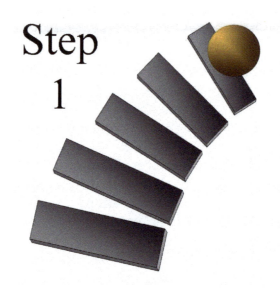

A review of " The 5 Step Plan"

STEP 1 – Sample the lifestyle. Learn to sail.

Experience living aboard; be sure you are sharing a common vision of the cruising dream, so you can arrive at a mutual decision of if, how, and when to proceed.

Take sailing lessons. Attend Boat shows and seminars.
Choose a sailing school that fits your style. Some of the schools offer a fleet of charter boats on some of the finest cruising grounds, so that you can get started living your dream.

Boat shows not only let you peek at beautiful boats, they offer a vast selection of seminars on various topics, such as planning a cruise, anchoring techniques and basic diesel maintenance.

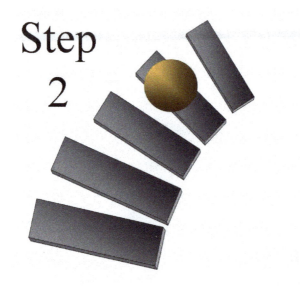

STEP 2 – Get time on the water.

Go day sailing. Try racing.
Nothing replaces time on the water actively sailing, learning to feel and sense the environment of wind and wave, and how a sailboat responds to them. We recommend joining as crew on races at a local sailing club where you can watch and learn from others' mistakes before you captain your own boat.

Charter on your own
At this point, you should have your Bareboat Charter Certification. It's time to solo. Try joining a flotilla for your first charter. A flotilla provides a "safety net," where you captain your own charter boat, but you follow the group of boats with a guide on the lead boat. Try various different models of boats, monohull aft cockpit, monohull center cockpit or catamaran. After all, how will you know if you want a monohull or a catamaran if you haven't sailed both of them, or sampled living aboard.

Go new places. Build your experience. Try out different locations to gain experience in a variety of wind and sea conditions. Different seasons produce very different wind and sea conditions. You should gradually experience larger seas and heavier winds to determine how well you deal with the changing situations. This may also help you set real goals for how far offshore you plan to sail with your partner. In other words, will you truly be crossing oceans or staying near the coast?

Step 3

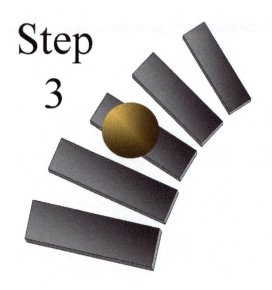

Mega yacht or 45 foot cruising sloop, choose wisely.

STEP 3 Buy the right boat.

Key points to consider before you shop. The budget, determine your intended use, bluewater or coastal cruising, new or used, monohull or catamaran, what yacht features to look for and understand what compromises you may need to make. Examine other factors, such as insurance, financing or options such as yacht ownership in charter company fleets like the Catamaran Company, Horizon, Moorings, Sunsail or TMM.

The purchase process. Use a buyer's broker to help you find the right boat and to guide you through the purchase process. When it comes time to negotiate the deal, the broker serves as the go between for the buyer and seller. Select a surveyor who will give you the real appraisal (bargaining tool), so that you don't overpay for the boat.

Important checklist for after the purchase. Once you agree to accept the vessel and complete the transaction, you need to: have a name for the boat, decide on registration or documentation, select where you will keep the boat during the transition for living aboard. You need insurance immediately. Also set aside funds for taxes and to address items in need of repair found on the survey, as well as funds for ongoing maintenance.

Step 4

Learn to fly the spinnaker.

STEP 4 – Learn your boat.

Get familiar with your boat and its systems. The modern cruising boat is equipped with many systems from the engine to the generator, to the galley and head, which allow you to live aboard with all the modern conveniences. However, it is more like managing a small city than a campground. Learn how each system operates and how to maintain it. Go cruising disconnected from shore power for at least two weeks. After your practice cruises, you may have to go back to the dock to add or change some of the equipment. Practice voyage planning. Think about where you want to cruise, invest in cruising guides and charts.

Step 5

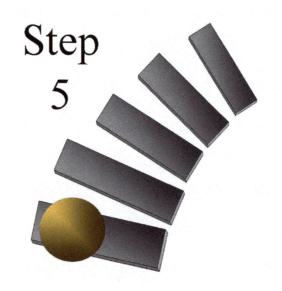

Walter and Jeanette learning radar.

STEP 5 – Get advanced training.

Continue your education with advanced training.

Take formal weather courses with instruction on understanding National Weather Service broadcast data. Learn to prepare forecasts from this data. Learn how to read and interpret the National Oceanic Atmospheric Administration (NOAA) raw weather data so that you can do your own voyage planning. Practice forecasting the weather and checking your results. If your boat is equipped with a Single Side Band (SSB) you will need to get additional training on how to use it as well. You also may need to take a course on radar navigation. Give yourselves time to practice nighttime operation on short passages close to homeport before you head off for distant shores.

What our clients say about us!

"We just wanted to again say thank you for a magical weekend. ... Jonathan and I were so impressed by your range of incredible skills from the technical and mechanical sailing skills to your ease with people and wonderful communication abilities. Your cooking was wonderful, your stories were entertaining, and your instruction was patient and gently paced.
The ocean, the bay, the evening sail, the introductory navigational and sailing tips acquired, the still night waters, the peaceful cove anchorage, the playful dolphins, the bright stars, and the gentle breezes were sublime. Thank you for graciously showing us all these wonders."
Michele and Jonathan on Step 1: Learning the Lifestyle

"Connie and I can't say 'thank you both' enough to make a dent in the appreciation and gratitude we feel towards you. Giving someone the ability to participate in something they really enjoy isn't quite like giving someone a kidney, but it is close."
Connie & Brendan on Step 2: Time on the water, new places

"...the biggest and most important thank you should go to the two of you. The seminar is well planned, helpful, interesting. You are great teachers! It was time well spent for us. So glad we were part of it. We took another look at the Endeavor 42 in Placida on our way to the airport. Again thanks for all of your help!"
Margaret and Jim on Step 3: Boat Selection and Shopping

"Woo Hoo!! Major accomplishment yesterday for Debbie! I *gently* docked at the pump out station without mishap!! I even had to do it in reverse! Thanks so much for the lessons!"
Debbie & Rob on Step 4: Learning their boat
"Chick-A-Lou" Beneteau 43

"It's been an exciting two years for us, especially our first year living aboard Cerulean. I can honestly say that without Jeff and Jean, I could not have made the transition from suburban homeowner to live aboard cruiser."
Robin & Chris on Step 5: Out Cruising!
"Cerulean" Catalina 445

"Each new harbor, new tight passage, new anchorage, we get stronger. We've grown a lot these past 17 days and have come to the realization we can do this and we enjoy it! You opened up a new world for us and we will always be in your debt. Fair winds"
Jim & Marcie on Step 5: Out Cruising!
"Island Jim" Island Packet 380

"What a super job you two are doing teaching couples to do what you are passionate about. I know they are getting the best advice when they learn from you. Warm regards"
Peter Trogdon
President, Weems & Plath
Marine Supply Annapolis, MD.

"I was asked to attend Jeff & Jean's 'Two Can Sail' seminar this weekend at Lakewood Yacht Club in Texas. As usual, they did an excellent job and have a unique perspective on the concept of couples cruising. Their presentation was balanced, informative and fun. They are going a long way to answering the myriad questions couples have when they are making the big decisions about buying a boat and moving aboard"
Steve Bowden
President, Sea-Tech Systems

About the authors

Jeff and Jean assist couples in realizing sailing dreams with their company Two Can Sail. They work with one couple at a time to provide cruising lifestyle consulting, including (but not limited to), buyer's brokers assisting with boat shopping, purchase, surveying and personal training aboard the couple's boat.
Jean is a Society of Accredited Marine Surveyors (SAMS) Accredited Marine Surveyor (AMS) and is American Boat & Yacht Council (ABYC) Standards Certified. Both Jeff and Jean are 100GT Masters and American Sailing Association (ASA) Certified Sailing Instructors. Together, they have over 60 years of experience operating over 180 different models of sailboats, including dozens of cruising catamarans. They have cruised extensively in the Caribbean, the East coast of the U.S. from Maine to Texas, as well as the Yucatan coast of Mexico, specializing in navigating the Gulf Stream. Jeff holds an Electrical Engineering (BSEE) & Computer Engineering degree and has worked with almost all forms of electronic navigation.
Jeff and Jean have a passion to share their experience of cruising through a variety of sailing offerings focused on Couples training.

CPSIA information can be obtained
at www.ICGtesting.com
Printed in the USA
BVHW020559150521
607159BV00004B/47